Further Darkness & Light
A collection of poetry

Compiled & Edited

by

Paul B Morris

To Maelei, Best wishes & good luck x
2019

nOthing BOOKS

Copyright © 2018 Nothing Books Publishing

Edited by Paul B Morris

All rights reserved. No part of this book may be reproduced in any form or by any means, except by inclusion of brief quotations in a review, without permission in writing from the publisher.

Each author retains copyright of their own individual poetry, though, no part of this book may be reproduced in any form or by any means, except by inclusion of brief quotations in a review, without permission in writing from the publisher

This book is a work of poetic fiction. The characters and situations in this book are as a result of creative imagination and are not real. No resemblance is intended between these characters and any persons living, dead or undead.

This book is sold subject to the condition that it shall not, by way of trade or otherwise, be lent, resold, hired out otherwise circulated without the publisher's prior consent in any form other than that in which it is published.

Published in Great Britain in 2018 by Paul B Morris, Nothing Books Publishing, West Midlands, UK

Cover photography and mosaic by David Nicholls © of David Nicholls Art. Cover design and arrangement by Paul B Morris © of nOthing BOOKS.

ISBN:
ISBN-13: 978-1986671675
ISBN-10: 1986671674

Thank you to ………

You, for buying this book and supporting MIND, a fantastic charity who do so much for mental health in the United Kingdom.

Every amazing poet soul who has contributed to this incredible book, giving your work freely, in the hope that others may benefit.

MIND for doing what they do.

David Nicholls, for believing in me and creating an incredible piece of art which now adorns the cover of this book.

My family.

Helen, my incredible Wife, who has supported me throughout everything. Without you I am nothing. I love you so much!

Paul xxx

From all over the world

people share their poetry

through hope, love and peace

Paul B Morris

Contents

Rain Man – Alan Wilkinson	7
Puppet Master – Alan Wilkinson	8
New Beginning – Andrew Lennon	9
Hide Behind a Smile – Andrew Lennon	10
Stress Blanket – Andrew Lennon	11
I'll Write – Andrew Mutaawe	12
The Broken Shell – Angel LaVey	13
#Me Too – Angel LaVey	14
Bubblegum Bubble – Angie Payne	15
Sea of Society – Angie Payne	18
Hurt – Becky Narron	19
I'm Here – Becky Narron	20
Devine – Callum Chalmers	21
Forever Yours – Callum Chalmers	22
Within – Calum Chalmers	23
I Only Endure This Way – Catalina George	24
A Moment of Absence – Catalina George	25
Soul Solitude – Chad Gooding	27
A Way – Chad Gooding	28
Forsaken – Chad Gooding	29
Invisible Illness – Chloe Gilholy	30
I Win Everyday – Chloe Gilholy	32
A Shadow Follows Me – Claire Johnson	33
Knocked me Down – Claire Victoria Sutton	34
I Am Just Me – Claire Victoria Sutton	35
Beat Me – Claire Victoria Sutton	37
Morning – C. R. Resetarits	38
Nighttime – C. R. Resetarits	39
A Cliché is Stalking Me – Dale Parnell	40
Reasons to Smile #1 – Dale Parnell	42
Heads or Tales – Dale Parnell	43
Stand Alone – David Nicholls	44
Need – David Nicholls	46
Darkness & Light – David Nicholls	48
I Remember. Do You? – David W. Ruswaza Amooti	49
The Patriot – David W. Ruswaza Amooti	50
The Courtrooms – David W. Ruswaza Amooti	51

Shadowed Forests of the Past – Denise Dianaty	53
Shackled Souls – Denise Dianaty	55
Mother Lost – Denise Dianaty	56
Through the Black Hole and Back – Denny Reader	57
Life is a Thorny Black Rose – Denny Reader	58
The Nobody – Denny Reader	60
Make it Stop – Derek Dohren	61
Games Night – Derek Dohren	63
Untitled – Derek Dohren	65
That's Life – Des Mannay	66
A Pearl Amongst Swine – Des Mannay	67
Another Day – Des Mannay	68
Faithful – Dominic Mulgrew	69
Stressed – Dominic Mulgrew	70
Taking Chances – Dominic Mulgrew	71
Could be the Elves – Donna Meyer	73
Ten Thousand Fireflies – Donna Meyer	74
Bel13ve – D. S. Scott	75
(Maybe) I Should Forgive Myself – D. S. Scott	76
Patcher Upper – Dwane Reads	77
On the Complex – Dwane Reads	78
Darkness Moves Away – Eduardo Escalante	79
A Different Kind of Glass – Eduardo Escalante	80
Before – Edward Ferrari	81
After – Edward Ferrari	82
Mind Your Language – Emerson Wilkes	83
Tonight – Faleeha Hassan	84
Empty Poem – Faleeha Hassan	85
I Ask You – Gail Moran Slater	87
100 Words – Gail Moran Slater	88
You – Geoff Bennett	89
Worthy Burden – Geoff Bennett	90
The Things I Wished I Didn't Do – Gerald Kells	91
Wretched Poet – Gerald Kells	92
Synthesis – Ian Davies	93
The Final Performance of the Great Ridiculous Hermaphrodite – Ian Davies	95
Now and Then I Have to Come Face to Face – Ian Davies	97
At the Window – Ian Henery	99
Black Country Water – Ian Henery	100

Liar – J Snow	101
Nothing – J Snow	107
Barricade – J Snow	108
I Chose You – J. L. Lane	109
All-Day Suckers – James Michael Shoberg	111
False Tooth – James Michael Shoberg	112
Tired – James Michael Shoberg	113
A Birdless Cage – Jason Conway	114
Shipwrecked – Jason Conway	118
Beach of my Soul – Jason N Smith	119
Darkness is a Womb – Jason N Smith	120
Can You Hear Us Calling? – Jason N Smith	121
Believe in Self Belief – Jan Hedger	122
Been a Poor Year – Jan Hedger	123
Knife – Jean Aked	124
Slumber – Jean Aked	125
Waffling – Jean Aked	126
Have You Ever Felt -- Jennie Barron	127
Luminous – Jennie Barron	129
Within These Red Walls – Jozilea Faulkner	130
Find Inspiration in Emptiness – Jozilea Faulkner	135
Every Ghost Will Return – Jude Brigley	136
Exfiltration – Jude Brigley	137
Black Dog – James WF Roberts	138
Do You? – James WF Roberts	140
Brooklyn Soothsayer – Judy Shepps Battle	142
Stone Archway - Karen Horsley	143
White Light Shadow – Karen Horsley	144
For Z and L – Kathryn Carter	145
And She Just Sang/Caught in the Crossfire – Kate Edwards-Kearney	146
Would You Really See Me? – Kitty Kane	147
Crash Course Love – Kristina V Griffiths	148
Recall of a Love – Kristina V Griffiths	149
Little Fires – LM Cooke	151
The Watcher – LM Cooke	152
Sonnet 2231 – Linda Angel	153
There – Linda Angel	154
No Time for Goodbyes – Leanne Cooper	155
This is Not a Cry for Help – Leanne Cooper	156

Jade – Leanne Cooper	157
The Butcher, Baker and Candlestick Maker – Leanne Locker	158
Reality Check – Lesly Finn	159
What Can't Be Cured – Lesly Finn	160
Valkyrie Dreamer – Linda M. Crate	161
Flood of Light – Linda M. Crate	162
Turning Nightmares to Dust – Linda M. Crate	163
In My Dreams – Lynn White	164
Sunrise – Lynn White	165
Sometimes There is Magic – Lynn White	166
Lost – Marianne Burgess	167
So Lonely – Marion Feasey	168
Life and Death – Marion Feasey	169
Mr Hide – Matthew Cash	170
Last Night I Said "I Love You" – Matthew Cash	171
Sinister Grins – Matt Humphries	172
What We Like? – Matt Humphries	173
The Sands of Time Divide – Matt Humphries	174
Emily, Come and Take Your Place in the Human Race – Matt Nunn	175
Everyday Disappointment – Matt Nunn	176
Bird Feeder – Maureen Weldon	177
Resistance – Michael Carter	178
Salt – Michael Carter	179
Snowfall – Michael Carter	180
Beneath the Shallows – Michael Cronogue	181
Love Conquers Hate – Michael Cronogue	182
Unselfish Love – Nerisha Kemraj	183
Immobile – Nerisha Kemraj	184
Night Sadness – Norbert Gora	185
World Full of Anxiety – Norbert Gora	186
The Unforgiven – Paul Beech	187
I Hope – Paul B Morris	188
Disconnected – Paul B Morris	189
Down – Paul B Morris	191
Thoughtful Dread – Paul John Elias	192
Hidden Shame – Paul John Elias	193
I Need You to See Me – Paul Raynsford	195
There Was a Time – Paul Raynsford	197
My Fight With Depression – Paul Raynsford	198

Embers – Pippa Bailey	200
Flying with the Music – Rachel Arnold	201
Treasures of the Mind – Rachel Arnold	203
At Peace – Rachel Melia	204
Overwrought – Rachel Melia	205
Little Me – Rachel Melia	206
Parts of Me – Red Gibson	207
Impaled – Red Gibson	208
I Can Feel (Assault Survival) – Red Gibson	209
Pay the Ghosts – Richard Archer	210
Wish Fulfilment – Richard Archer	211
I'm Smiling on the Inside? – Richard Archer	212
Loving an Illusion – Richard Beevor	213
World Flowers – Richard Beevor	214
The Friend in my Head – Richard Beevor	215
Agency for the Lost Souls – Richard Proffitt	217
Dear Counsellor – Richard Proffitt	218
Home Sanity Kit – Richard Proffitt	220
The Weight of Space – Roz Weaver	221
Solitude – Roz Weaver	222
One for Sorrow – Roz Weaver	223
Lost – Ryan Woods	224
Fifty Shades of Mediocrity – Ryan Woods	227
Next Stop….Nowhere! – Ryan Woods	229
After the Rain – Sahana Mukherjee	231
Sending my Father Away – Sahana Mukherjee	232
Dream Stealer – Sarah Battison	233
Jagged Blankets of Depression – Sarah Battison	234
Destruction – Sarah Battison	240
Dirty Thoughts – Sarah Dale	241
Twisting and Breaking – Sarah Dale	242
The Ice Cave – Shaun Gurmin	243
Black Tears – Shaun Gurmin	245
Delhi 2004 – Sravani Singampalli	247
Life is a Glass of Coke – Sravani Singampalli	248
Front Page of the Express and Star – Stevie Quick	249
That my Name – Stevie Quick	250
What Does it Mean to be a Human? – Sunayna Pal	251
The Flood – Taylor Bain	252

Flame – Taylor Bain	253
Social Anxiety – Taylor Bain	254
Eclipsed – Tina Cole	255
Shell – Tina Cole	256
Infamy – Tina Manthorpe	257
Lindow Man – Tina Manthorpe	258
LePays Noir – William A Douglas Davies	260
Just Before – William A Douglas Davies	261
L'Addition – William A Douglas Davies	262
Paranoid – Xtina Marie	263
We'll Rendezvous – Xtina Marie	265
His Muse – Xtina Marie	267
The Parcel – Yolanda Barton	269
Apocalypse, Possibly – Yolanda Barton	271
Disco Tent – Z D Dicks	274
Unseen Entity – Z D Dicks	275
Portrait – Z D Dicks	276
Bouteille – Zoe Alford	277
Gregor – Zoe Alford	278

Rain Man
by Alan Wilkinson

If your first thought when sun turns to rain is shelter me,
I don't think you understand that you can swim in a stellar sea,
You enjoy the warmth of the sun yet fail to see the raindrops' beauty,
A billion miniature oceans falling to the Earth.

You'd rather hide from the storm than be engulfed by its passion,
You would spend all of your money on umbrellas to save your hair and cheap fashion,
That is where you and I differ, it is you who makes your own Hell on Earth,
You know the cost of things, I know only what things are truly worth.

Puppet Master
by Alan Wilkinson

You spend your years living as a puppet,
You never see the puppeteer but feel the pull of twine,
Controlling your every action, movement, decision, even your mind,
Allowing limited freedom with surgical precision.
From birth 'til death your path governed from above,
Not by a god but a power who does not know love,
Dragged through your life as a slave on a chain,
The puppeteer will not allow you to use your brain.
So who is pulling the strings?
You're not allowed to look,
Do as your told, follow the rule book.
From beyond the horizon, just out of view,
The puppeteer tweaks and twitches strings to control you,
You have to make a choice one day soon,
Do I live my life guided by hidden hands?
Or do I sharpen my mind to cut through these hidden bands?
Make your choice well, break free of chains and locks,
Before the puppeteer puts you one last time in your box.

New Beginning
by Andrew Lennon

I wish you could see in my head,
know how I much I want to quit.

I wake up every single day,
saying that 'I'm done with this shit'.

When afternoon comes around,
work and stress take their toll.

I think about another round,
just one more drink and that's all.

But I'm done with that stuff for good.

I'm finished and I'm getting sober.

I raise my head, take off my hood.

My journey's starting, it's not over.

**Hide Behind a Smile
by Andrew Lennon**

Depression wears a smiling face,
I know that, that seems out of place.
It's easier to run and hide,
Than show people what's locked inside.

A face may show a cheerful grin,
That just covers what's within.
But you can see through its disguise,
If you look into someone's eyes.

Stress Blanket
by Andrew Lennon

Stress is like a blanket.
It covers you and makes it hard to breathe,
you can't see a way out, so you kick and punch and sometimes,
end up hurting the people close to you that are trying to help.

When you listen and calm yourself,
the blanket is slowly removed.
Your vision clears, and you see the person that helped you remove it.
Then all is well again.

I'll Write
by Andrew Mutaawe

I'll write
Like I have no tomorrow,
Like I have only a few seconds
to write a witless will,
leaving my wife the bottle
and my son, the pen!
I'll write
like I'm an aesthete,
with this violin sound in my ears
that'd let me run out of ink
Because it makes the words trickle,
like sweat out of my word bank!
I'll write like a journalist,
Ready to selflessly
surrender my emotions like a journal,
to all these ears waiting to chew
all the edible pieces of my
Poetic justice...
I'll write like an accountant
who's just been hired,
In a company soon falling
like autumn leaves to dry!
And if the inspiration is intact,
With this sound of the violin,
And my pen full of ink,
I'll write
and write
and write.

The Broken Shell
by Angel LaVey

I am not fine.
I say I am because that is the expected reply.
The social contract between two British people.
You ask out of a perceived obligation, not a genuine desire to know.
So, I keep the faith and the contract observed to the letter with all required punctuations in place.

I am not whole. I am almost gone, a ghost of who I once was; with nothing but a hazy recollection of how I left her so far behind.
Forever lost in time and space as our planet is always moving through both the undeniable truth that science has taught us all.

I am not in one piece; although I look like I am to the casual glance.
I am shattered into billions of pieces so tiny it would take a lifetime to count them all.
Too tired to even have the energy for this long running pretense to continue.
Cruelly abandoned by my faking skills in the eleventh hour; my failures further compounded by yet more failures.
My broken shell made more obvious in the harsh sunlight illuminating it for all to behold.

#Me Too
by Angel LaVey

The problem lies with them not you
You did not deserve to be assaulted
It was not your fault you did nothing wrong
Release the shame you have held onto
They are the ones that should be ashamed
Let's silence those who will victim blame
We are in this together regardless of
Gender, race or creed
Predators prey on anyone but we will no longer
excuse or accept it.

Join our army so we can end it and call out
those who attempt to excuse or enable it
We have shone a light into this murky
practice and yet we have only exposed
a fraction of the behaviours that are toxic
Harassment so frequent no day passes
Without it & that's without all the
rapes, murders and mutilations
Let's do better and teach each other
To respect, accept and believe in
the goodness that we all have inside.

Bubble-gum Bubble
by Angie Payne

I was planning on writing a new poem for today
But it never happened
I was too busy
Too busy having man flu
Too busy with the snot
The snot that gets into your head
And you can't think of anything
Because it's just there
It's like you've blown a bubble-gum bubble
And the bubble has taken over your head
And its gets bigger and bigger
Till you can't think of anything
All you can see is the pink fluffy bubbliness bubble
Of the bubble-gum bubble in your head.

But Anyway I digress
I was planning on writing a new poem for today
But I was too busy
Too busy at work
I work in mental health
I work with students
Students come to see me with their mental health problems
And most of them
Most of them
It's because something's happened to them

So they might have been abused
Might have been that Uncle that slipped into his room
At 3 in the morning
And touched him inappropriately
And it's messed him up
And now he has to do a degree
But he can't sleep at night
Because he keeps thinking of that Uncle
The Uncle who came into his room at 3 in the morning

He goes to the doctor
The Doctor says he has anxiety, depression and PTSD
No shit Sherlock
Wouldn't you be ill if that happened to you Mr Doctor?

So anyway
He's got 3 essays to do
But he can't do the essays
Because he can't concentrate
He can't concentrate
Because he's exhausted
He's having flashbacks,
He can't sleep
He's awake at 3 in the morning
Shaking, Sweating
He can't eat
He thinks if he eats
He will get fat
And if he gets fat
He will hate himself even more
So he doesn't eat

So now
He's labelled Anorexic
So now he is told he has
Anxiety
Depression
PTSD
And Anorexia
What is he meant to do?

But anyway
I digress
He's got to get his essays done
If he doesn't get his essays done
He will fail the year
If he fails the year
He won't get the degree

And if he doesn't get the degree
He might not get the job he wants
And if he doesn't get the job he wants
He may be viewed by society
As a failure
And all because
And all because
Some paedophile couldn't control himself at 3 in the morning.

But Anyway I digress
I was planning on writing a new poem for today
But I was too busy
I was too busy at work
Busy at work and having man flu
With the bubble-gum head
So the bubble-gum head
And the busy at work
And walking the dog
And making the dinner
And the bubble-gum head

So now I am here
And this is my poem.

Sea of Society
by Angie Payne

I am rocking in this sea of society.
The wave pulls me under
So I am part of the minority.

I am pummelled by unspoken laws
Told to close all my thoughts
And ridiculed by politicians
Who have hoodwinked the majority?

I have fallen down so fast
That I've become a product of
My own self-fulfilling prophecy.
As I am engulfed by the suited and booted nine to five drones
Who are creating my anxiety?

With their ignorance is bliss
Misinformed compliancy
And their love for shopping
And media notoriety.

Yes I have a job sir.
Yes I am a slave to the printed paper just like you.
But I have no respect for this misguided authority,
Who tell us what to do and how to behave?
And who we should love and that we must cooperate
With corrupt corporations and murdering dictators
And accept inequality and become a wage slave.
So you are deluded sir if you think we are truly free
As we are all rocking sir, in this sea of society.

Hurt
by Becky Narron

The hurt inside is killing me
Isn't the way it's to be
The love for me is gone
You left me to carry on

I don't want to breathe
I do not want to live
Crawl away deep inside
Nevermore to feel alive

My soul is now crushed
My brain has turned to mush
You are gone pain lives on
Tomorrow is a new dawn

I don't want to give up
I will not ever let-up
I love your amazing heart
I promise to never depart

Forever and always
Your passion it does amaze
Lips that I want to kiss
Hands that I sure do miss

I cannot say enough
Losing you would be to tough
Please babe don't ever go
Without you, life's a NO.

Hurt
by Becky Narron

The hurt inside is killing me
Isn't the way it's to be
The love for me is gone
You left me to carry on

I don't want to breathe
I do not want to live
Crawl away deep inside
Nevermore to feel alive

My soul is now crushed
My brain has turned to mush
You are gone pain lives on
Tomorrow is a new dawn

I don't want to give up
I will not ever let-up
I love your amazing heart
I promise to never depart

Forever and always
Your passion it does amaze
Lips that I want to kiss
Hands that I sure do miss

I cannot say enough
Losing you would be to tough
Please babe don't ever go
Without you, life's a NO.

Devine
by Calum Chalmers

There is a man his name Devine
He feeds upon this flesh of mine
And though I gently softly weep
It is my soul he longs to keep
He takes my flesh in gentilc slithers
And cooks themst up in time for dinners
And though he feasts on taboo meats
This choice of mine is saintly treats
Though my time will soon be near
He quickly indulges on mine ear
I know it's wrong, I know it's right
I know I'll die I will not fight.

Forever Yours
By Calum Chalmers

As light shines across soft petal roads,
Like a droplet from heaven, your beauty it glows,
And together we'll walk forever as one
To reach where the rainbows cross with the sun.

And as the blaze of our love burns evermore
I will gaze in your eyes and know that for sure
We will walk together forever as one
To reach where the rainbows cross with the sun.

Within
By Calum Chalmers

An endless scream beats me from within.
Fingers scratch behind eyes as palms do best to blind me.
Venom pours down throat to drown lungs in their animosity.
Lone cries stifled by fear, anger washed beside me.
Alone I pray....
Alone I pray.

I Only Endure This Way
by Catalina George

Whenever my brain strays off
like a mad dog leaving its pack behind
poetry separates worries from light
it fills this crumpled heart back into its
shape
of expression and beauty
Whenever I ache with the struggle
jolts of pain shredding flesh away from soul
muscles tensed with the fear of a wounded animal
you pull me back to you
to the safety of
your embracing strength
Whenever despair chomps its way back
through time
a bad dream of solid nothingness
when walls seem to grow heads of hissing serpents
when time collapses within like an erupting volcano
I endure by this only
I speak again in the humming sounds
of poetry
the better shade of my flickering soul
I hold on to you my rock
my shelter my better side of love.

A Moment of Absence
by Catalina George

The blind spot unfolds behind the curtains
of grey light
to catch the day in its grasp
just when everything seemed to shape
in the corner of the eye

you move too quick
from eyes rubbing to phone checking
from coffee to getting your boots on

from thought to un-thought
the wheels brutalise the morning air
while birds still catch their first trills
gloves on
laptop tripod water bottle in the back of the car
yesterday's worries
brewing well-hidden
a double weight under the softness of the skin
the voice ruptures the moment
the rush
shatters the heart
you burst into thousands of pieces of
mirrored shards
of reality

you still think nothing is happening
yet

you drive straight into the next pile of
sketches from the future
you don't even see
you did not even check
before your hands moved
your body acted
in absence

a moment lost in the time of
what we could do
if we were here.

Soul Solitude
by Chad Gooding

I must be destined to toil here forever
All alone
No soft spot for me to land
Only stone
The ticks of time tiptoeing up on me
By myself I remain, where else would
I be

So much of this all I believe should
Be shared, but to find someone for me
I would not dream to dare

The end draws in closer now with each labored breath
No longer shall I be alone, I go now with death.

A Way
by Chad Gooding

Forever and always
A fraudulent swear
Left in these small days
Said you'd be there
Cold, cheated life
Is mine to behold
Pure, awful strife
Alone to grow old
Edged, fined pain
Slices me by day
Tempted draining vein
Seems a prudent way

Forsaken
by Chad Gooding

I'll shake your hand
when we meet upon that green
you've been left to self-destruct
never heard never seen
Tossed aside as a child's old toy
shown indifference to wounded love
ignorance for forgotten joy
Most valiant knight willing and able
stripped of place at Uncle Sam's table
we are brothers, I will welcome you always
forsaking all others

Invisible Illness
by Chloe Gilholy

Who gave you those scratches?
Did you hurt yourself?
What gave you get those cuts?
Stop cutting yourself!
Where did you get bump from?
Stop hitting yourself!
Why don't you see a doctor?
Stop beating yourself up!

I
CAN'T
JUST
STOP

You're all so focused on what you can see
Instead of thinking about what you can't
Doctor said there's nothing wrong with me
Because I resemble a florescent plant

I sleep through the pain
And wake up in pain
My bones aren't broken
My ligaments are in tact
It's all in my head.

I want to get rid of this
horrific invisible illness
that rapes me at night
calls me names and says
the world would be better
without me

I want to prove it wrong
I want it to stop
But there are triggers
In every corner

One thing out of place
One tiny crack
Makes my world explode
Shattered tears
Hailing echoes that
Only I can hear

Anything to fill
this perpetual
emptiness

this is where I say goodbye...

I Win Everyday
by Chloe Gilholy

I'm not doing this anymore,
beating myself up silly.
It's an absolute chore –
Keeping this canned self-pity.

I'm one with the phoenix.
Soaring from coal ashes,
And conquer corrupt politics
Ready to face the classes.

Now, I've become Babylon
The light will never go away.
And from this moment on:
I win everyday.

A Shadow Follows Me
by Claire Johnson

A shadow follows me
Like a dark cloud
Constantly hovering over my pounding head
It shakes my whole body
And steals the air from my lungs
It squeezes my heart, making it race to keep beating
It never leaves my side
Sometimes it's farther away
Like a cat following my every footstep and always ready topounce
And other times its right by my side, gripping my shoulders tightly
And making every move terrifying
There were times when it seemed to disappear
Only to return suddenly and more powerful than before.

Knocked me Down
by Claire Victoria Sutton

You hit me
you beat me
you knocked me to the floor
If you didn't get what you wanted
you would do it ten times more
You never showed you loved me
you never showed you cared
If I had a problem
you were never there
You would swear when you were angry
or shout when you were mad
We never had any good times
they were always really bad
You would control me
then beat me black and blue
And that's the day
I closed the door
and walked away from you.

I Am Just Me
by Claire Victoria Sutton

I have mental problems
I must be bad
I can't be a nice person
I must be mad
They point
They shout
They laugh
They swear
Thinking I am different
But they don't care

But I am me
I cannot change
I am still human
Not insane

I have feelings
I am full of emotion
I cannot help who I am
I wish there was a potion
To make it go away
For me to smile
To have lovely thoughts
If even just for a while

Thoughts and feelings
Whirling around my mind
I ask myself, why
No answers I can find
In a crowded room
I still feel alone
I live with just me, myself
All on my own

I would love to go out
And meet the world

But they say I'm weird
A freak I'm told
But they don't know me
They second guess
Thinking my life is screwed up
And I am just a mess

I want to be happy
And smile again
Maybe relax
Just now and then
I want to go out
To sing and to dance
I want this world
To give me a chance

Beat Me
by Claire Victoria Sutton

You hit me, you beat me
You knocked me to the floor
When they asked me what happened
I said, I walked into a door
Never knowing what was next
Not knowing what's in store
If you didn't get what you wanted
You would do it ten times more

Why do you keep hurting me
What is it that I have done
Every single day
Do you just do this for fun

Your twisted eyes of evil
The smirk upon your face
Can't take this pain in silence
My hearts in the right place

You would grab me, hurt me
Throw me to the ground
Leave me to suffer
Until the time that I am found

Shaking, trembling, petrified in fear
Crying in silence
Every time that you come near

Feeling so lonely
And being on my own
Never feeling safe
Even in my own home

All these cuts and bruises
Getting more and more each day
Your explanation
I'm always in the way.

Morning
by C. R. Resetarits

In this light, empty, with singular view,
it seems a fine, old chair.
It is well-situated near conjoining walls --
whose angle augments the chair's
bread-loaf back, custard color, brioche-soft cushions.
And yet, hung above this lovely yellow chair,
a horrid little still life discomposes:
peon palette, situation arrière-garde.

Someone remarks -- as music pours
through teaspoon chimes,
muffled tenor of milky latte bowls,
rustle of newspapers and school satchels,
as hushed, poured voices fall side to side
like waterfalls in empyreal spins
(or suburban impish realms) --
and so, someone remarks
how that most capricious yellow chair
well-placed and ever-ardent to attend
is wrecked, made something else again
by that tricky mess above
(like a brilliant egg spoilt by sloppy hash).
Poor thing is left to evoke a burdensome emptiness,
that chair in light of that hovering blemish
seems a threat to this lovely morning space.
Yet even as we sip, nibble scones, and mull,
a hapless, droopy-drawered child sits
with aplomb and squeaking springs
in the doomed yellow chair,
below the infantile swirl of paint and
he is as suddenly as breaking yolk
the Lilliput king and
tragic art is rather beckoning and
the yellow chair is suddenly thread-bare rare,
Pooh-old, new and old and ours again.

Nighttime
by C. R. Resetarits

Our little whorl rings your office hoping
you might be free for lunch. You are and
we meet at his favorite sandwich shop
to munch and mull and yield before the child.

We smile, laugh, seem so simply whole.
We are at such times a clan,
at other times a clash.

Even so, we are a genteel, Gordian kink,
provocation anchored in shades of sun-
beams and roily-woolley clouds, nursery
foils for harms unseen until our evenings
slide into bloodlet wakes and nighttime
twists and we play tourniquet to the vast horizons
of this our most beloved begottedness.

Yet, while we squirm, our child
is fast a-cobbling dreams of rubbish and spark
when midnight sends us to our cots, to lie in wait,
besieged, beheld by the surety of his awesome sleep.

A Cliché is Stalking Me
By Dale Parnell

Listen
Can you hear it?
Behind the endless, inane, too-loud babble
The screeching, retching laughter of a hundred-thousand voices
It's there
Calling to you
Insisting you find silence
So it can whisper in your ear
You know what it is
You've met him before
And so it seems
A cliché is stalking me

Look there
Can you see it?
Behind the smiles and the pained effort
A sickness, a cold dark lump of nothing that's slowly sinking in
It's there
Waiting for you
Stealing your sleep
And showering you with lethargic kisses
You know what this is
You've felt it before
And so it seems
A cliché is stalking me

Wait
Can you feel it?
The white hot impatient rage
The broken, helpless grief for everything and nought
It's here
Upon you
The darkening skies
The shadow of a huge black hound

And so it seems
A cliché has found me

Swallow
Can you taste it?
Behind Mondays foil a white oval pill
A safety line / a crutch, clean air / your prison cell
It's here
To comfort you
The chemical imbalance redressed
Your new routine, your new best friend
You know what this is
You've been here before
And so it seems
The cliché is me.

Reasons to Smile #1
By Dale Parnell

Tired and stiff
Legs, and back
And forth to a toilet
Too cramped.
A flash,
Did you see it?
A glimpse through the winding
Lanes that we follow
Downhill to the sea.
I can see it
Shining.
The sea is shining
All for me
And for you sat beside me
Say you saw the waves first,
And claim your win.

Heads or Tails
By Dale Parnell

Heads I win, tails I lose
Flipping a coin so my brain can choose.

Which way will I go today,
Happy or sad?
How low will I feel today?
How tragic, how mad?

What's wrong with you mate?
Turn that frown upside down.
But I'm not a court jester,
Or a carnival clown.

Monday was even,
Tuesday the same,
But this morning I'm broken,
I don't like this game.

In the grit filled headache,
In the tears that I cry,
In the stares from a stranger,
In the things I can't try,
In all of the empty, blackened thoughts that will not leave me
Sits the last dying ember of hope for tomorrow.

Heads I win, tails I lose
The coin keeps on spinning,
Why can't I choose?

I Stand Alone
by David Nicholls

I stand alone

Where am I?
I'm not so sure
But many times
I have been here before

Desolate places

A wind swept plain
Bitter cold
Biting wind
Fingers numb, icy pain
Eyes sting with steely rain

A dry cracked desert
Barren like a forgotten womb
Scorching sun and stinging sand
Searing pain on blistered feet
Mile on mile of endless heat

A ship at sea
Icy water filled with dread
Bottomless depth
Waiting to take me down
Mermaids calling while I drown

A rocky shore
Waves crash across its slippery face
Booming sound to deafen ear
Salt cracked lips sing their pain
I wonder how I am here again

A darkened room
I silently wake
This time not alone

Warmth and love
Not cold and fear

Where am I?

I'm not so sure
But many times
I have been here before..

Need
by David Nicholls

I need to take myself away from this world
For a while
Remove body from reality
Shed skin of apparent familiarity
Rip up my normal life ticket
And peel off these robes of illusion
Run to the hills
And escape a land of delusion

I need to take flight
Spread my steely wings
Jump from this barren cliff
Fly free
Soar way above any misguided plight
Breathe new air
And live with the angels for a while
No falseness or deception
Bring down a hammer
And break free these shackles of abjection.

I need to smash these towers
And tear down the walls
Run a million miles
To shut out the fools
Cover my ears
To listen to the soft voice
That I tend to ignore
Let sweetness take me
To an avenue of trees
For nectar drips freely
As I lay quietly beneath the majestic
But once more as usual
I am torn from this peace

I need to break free from these iron bars
That are clamped like a vice above my head

Reach up
And pull myself amongst the stars
To find true peace
And gaze down through drifting cloud
While at rest
Amongst angels wings
Comfortable
For just a little while
With who I really am.

**Darkness & Light
by David Nicholls**

Isaiah 9:2 - The people who walk in darkness Will see a great light;
Those who live in a dark land, The light will shine on them.

To walk in darkness
And strive for light
To exist in a dark land
So fractured
A soulless plight
To lift heavy head from dusky ground
Stiff neck and creaking bones
Light is a grasp
Too far to reach
As Angels dust floats slowly down
Black rivers run like needle thread
Treacle tar through withered vein
The shadow horse moves
Across a dishevelled sky
Hollow footprints left in ashen ground
Feet retrace what's left behind
And a wanting ear waits
For an angels sound
But no golden trumpets come
And as human
We shuffle on
Through a grey cloud of life
For muffled pleasure
Seems little solace
Within
This great reasoning
Of
What we
Call
Life.

I Remember. Do You?
by David W. Ruswaza Amooti

In the wake of season
You formed the twig;
In the wreck of reason
You formed the bud
You my love.

In the emptiness of thought
You flowered and caught
The hollowness of my sight,
From the petals of your goodness
You my love.

In the guise of self
You bore the fruit
For the gust of our heart
And the gust of our lust
Gushed at last out from my thirst
You my love.

Of the kindness of your being
Of the likeness of your seeing
I saw the living
The living that made me
Made me think now
Of the cling we swing.

You my love
Now here we're
In the paths
Of life's long longing journey,
Jogging trotting trekking;
In arms of despair, we spare
For the care of our love;
Our children!

The Patriot
by David W. Ruswaza Amooti

How much with pain my heart -
Is tarred -and -feathered
How much in anguish my soul deeps
And plunges into the fathoms of the deepest sea
unfathomable-
How much shall my soul go reeling out?
To the high seas and gales of the turbulence
Like the fisherman's line into the unpredictable waters
How much shall I pour myself out?
To this nation ever unyielding to the cry of her own?
My heart has struck the bed and boulders
The sea hasn't been kind to my heart
Rent clean it has been
The blood gashes out afloat
The ship and the boat and the canoe
Are but stained with my meagre fluid
I neglected, left alone to the sharks and whales;
My life I give you my country.

The Courtrooms
by David W. Ruswaza Amooti

We cuddled in the blindest corner of the innermost room.
Deafening silence rang around us
Real ghost belfry bells
My ears itched, twitched and ached.
To sounds of the loud silence.
Nobody had bang my ears
Not in the last fortnight that I can remember
The same thing could have been happening in the main room
The judgment room so it seemed
A flicker of light radiating through the keyhole
Sending bubbles of ray-conjured ghosts
On the high ventilation-free walls;
Lock-click! went the jingle in the keyhole
We froze; the hour is up.
The sudden swing and sway of the dungeon door
The inflow and flooding of the room
With highly reflective beams left us blind.
Up! That was heard we all rose to the occasion;
None knew I'd go in first
When my cufflinks were unlocked my heart skipped and sunk.
Faint mummers could be heard in the courtroom.
The judgment seat; yes, the symbol
Of power and authority and mighty
Stood still in a radiance of awe and wonder
At the cite of it my legs gave way, I almost fainted
The centurion caught me midway.
The mahogany door- or it was
Behind the judgment throne swung open
The packed court swarmed up to join me
For I had been standing in the booth
All alone and along awaiting this horrible moment.
Here she enters with heavenly might
She could have been young
She could have been old who could tell
No introduction was made
The head gear in white

The cassock in brown
All covered to the nail
A judge of high office
The only visible face as gloomy as hell
Could be part of the proceedings
Could be part of human nature
Or the surrounding attire created mismatched elusions
Whatever, 'twas scary symbolism
Her I must face and today.
Whoever hit the table to signal sitting
I can't remember
Like the Mexican wave court sank into the pews. Silence.
In my seat-less cage still and stiff remained I.
My mind raced all the mileage of my memory
To and fro and quickly again many times
I have to answer charges for a case I haven't committed
Or is there a case I committed and forgot
The heart would answer back
With a resounding No. No crime committed.
But answering must I.
It's six months or so ago that I remember
Caught up in a police fracas with Mwana NCI
Like in a cross fire caught was l
Court is summoned to order the judge's voice is heard.
Prosecutor: Case file number zero one.
Attempt to overthrow legitimate government.
Defendant in dock, your Lordship.
I died! I woke up in the dark room again. Alone.
Waited for yet another knock-click in the keyhole;
That, never came.

Shadowed Forests of the Past
by Denise Dianaty

Bad old, dark places…
Places where my life no longer dwells…
Looking back upon the past…
That wasting, dark, drear past…
Come words from a long ago
Where my soul no longer cowers.

A place of wrenching loneliness
always on the edge of light,
waiting to drag me back…
back into its embrace….
I just kept trying to hold on,
trying to hold out for love;

But, every day that passed without it,
Loneliness lurked to overwhelm.
And, darker still, monsters lurked…
Monsters lurked at every… every turn…
Soul shattering dramas spun out
in relentless perversions of hope.

Until that pivotal moment…
that time when change began…
Change began and Hope was born…
Hope born anew within my breast.
In that Hope, on angel's breath…
An angel-friend led me forward.

She led me through the dark
and back to light and Faith.
I learned the true Me…
the truest Me I was meant to be
And learning Me, I learned Love.
Learning Love, I learned to love.

It's a truly blessed state... In brilliant shining sunlight...
A place of laughter and love and joy...
Such have I found for myself...
After the long, dark road through tortured,
Shadowed forests of the past.

Shackled Souls
by Denise Dianaty

A weak flesh for paltry failing hearts
Too human in this here and now
The soul stretching toward heaven
Clamouring for a return to the Divine
But unruly flesh, feeling too much
Turning toward the shadows
In immediacy of mortal pain
Chaining the eternal… imprisoned
Too worn by such earthly need
So heavy with venal desires
Shackled souls weighted for Hell.

Mother Lost
by Denise Dianaty

In her young heart she loved
She wanted nothing more than to give love
She wanted children, a crowd about her
A song unique for each bright star
She loved her babies, sang her joy
Gently cuddled and held them safe
Three times with ease brought to life
Blest gifts, her fair headed delights
Then came the fourth, hard fought
Ripped from her body, at last
With all her might, the last dram of heart
At last, brought through alive

Why to look upon that face
What darkness left behind
A burden, a sorrow, each shining bright face
Take and take and take and take
Nothing more she wants now, save death
Oh no, say the doctors, the nurses, the society
Lock her away till she learns to lock down her pain
Don't guide her back through to the light
No more songs, joyless duty and burden are hers
Her anger, her blackened soul,
Locked behind closed doors
It's not our concern
Send her home to her babies
No matter their plight

Through The Black Hole and Back
by Denny Reader

Up to the highest heights, deep through the darkest, deadliest caverns,
To the Abyss of the human Soul, within the planes of Heavenly control,
Where Angels sing your name, where Gods grace your path,
Where the Mind is transcended from All ego and
suffering. Then....

Back to the Dark Depths, back to Demons and Mind parasites,
Tormenting and Possessing. Lost. Gone. Hidden. Destroyed.
The Self escapes, your mind gone, your soul stolen,
And only evil, Hell and Darkness remains,

Then. The Sun Rises again, and I begin to float, Fly,
I see and I witness, life after life pass before my eyes,
Like connecting to the collective memory of the Earth, humanity and the Universe, I am guided, held, redeemed, reprieved, I travel across the Universe and see Amazing things, The Inner Worlds, Life in so many kinds,
Knowledge, Experience; Then...

Gone. Destroyed. Broken down, I fall to pieces, only left to crawl upon some lost sense of self, this time I am travelling the Underworld, where lost souls and Devils lurk, no light, no love,
Through the mist and back closer to common ground, I feel like I've lived a thousand Lives, a thousand Deaths and a thousand Pains,
I walk to the local shops, nothing seems changed, I step into the local pub,
And it's like the people there are still sipping on the same beer,
The people doing near exactly the same thing, - no upheavals here,
But Within me;

I have died, gone to Heaven and Hell, ventured a vast universe,
Seen the Light and the Dark, the in-between.
I have Lived a thousand Lives. I have felt a thousand Pains.

Life is a Thorny Black Rose
by Denny Reader

Bitter sweet, up and down, hurt and burnt…
Life Is a Thorny Black Rose,
Ecstatic, suicidal, manic, zombified;

Low, like an anchor into a bottomless sea,
High, Like a helium balloon floating endlessly upward,
'Knifes in the back', Can't get out of bed,
Wings guiding me forward out of the darkness and into
infinite light,

Expansive states of mind forever reaching into the depths of
consciousness, concepts of the Universe and Purpose,
Then Dead, like a rotten corpse, mouldy, stale,

I feel Lost, so lost, so lost…..
Life Is a Thorny Black Rose,

Into a boundless labyrinth I tread,
No way out, only through, but no clues, no clues, so lost,
Wall after wall, after wall, the odds stacked against me,
The World crumbling around me, suicide, sickness, death,
shadows,
But hope, new Life, Birth, Joy,
I trek and wander, and walk and walk,
Aeons seem to go by, lost, so lost wandering aimlessly it
seems,

Then I discover an immense trunk with thorns
Reaching up into the sky,
I climb and climb… Then at the top I discover it's a Rose,
A Jet Black Rose,
And inside I find a new hope,
I lie within its center, and Realise……..

Life Is A Thorny Black Rose.

Marvelous, So Beautiful, Complex, Yet Dark and Powerful,
Thorny, Painful, Yet Glowing so Radiantly, So Elegantly, So
Electric but Gloomy, Prickly, Spiky yet so Enigmatic,
It is an enigma,
It Is a Mystery............

Life Is A Thorny Black Rose.

The 'Nobody'
by Denny Reader

That person that silently struggles,
Upon the fringes of the social margins,
Frowned at, forgotten, misunderstood, undervalued;
That person; that person,
That, 'nobody'.

Your struggle, your battle, your everyday plight,
May not be so recognised by your peers around,
But your specialness, your sacredness, your individuality is there so true,
Those around and yourself fail to recognise your beauty,
Your worth, your justice, your presence,

Earth knows you so well, she knows all that walk upon her,
Even if so many others fall short to notice your kinship,
Believe me, if I know something,
I know we All have value, and you are no different in that vein.

You may feel hated, despised, forgotten and distrusted,
But being knows you,
And this universe has love for you,
The primal urge of existence is to experience,
You are always a part of that, no matter what,
Appreciate your life, your heart, yourself,
For there is beauty in you, no matter what others say or feel or do,
There is nobody, there is no nobody;

Nobody like you.

Make it Stop
by Derek Dohren

bathroom singer, ringer of fingertips
flinger of fingerprint tips
silicon chipped liposucked lips
full fat fried fish and chips
glutton dressed as mutton
consumer whore wrought
and store-bought with malice aforethought
effervescent omnipresence
built-in obsolescence

this international race
and national disgrace
face palm microphone drop
someone's gotta make it stop

subsumed consumer, consummate seducer
medically induced assumer
producer of intruding tumours
reducer of humorous juices
genuflect and resurrect
a circumspect Jesuit
reflect back onto it a deflecting conduit
inevitable complicity
irrevocable duplicity

this international race
and national disgrace
face palm microphone drop
someone's gotta make it stop

concealing appeaser, appealing teaser
squeezer and seizing policer
freezer of wheezy sneezing
healer of needy feeling
contactless interaction
contracted spinal column

a cosmic microcosm of global oppression
victims of circumstance
of unhappy happenstance

this international race
and national disgrace
face palm microphone drop
someone's gotta make it stop.

Games Night
by Derek Dohren

Garret window framing a planetary eclipse
seeking mediocrity in passing ships
a starburst bobbing head chameleon
an eagle eyed misguided authoritarian
handlebar moustache tailor made
florid complexion goose the chambermaid
and making a shifty makeshift observatory
it's Colonel Mustard in the conservatory
bashing that head with undue ceremony
holistic missile ballistic therapy.

and all the while seeking fellowship with
an overwatered peace lily and the remnants
of a takeaway Rogan Josh.

Clotted cream and Neolithic burial mounds
megaliths and ley lines over holy ground
a chunk of blue labradorite
an unidentified piece of chlorite
whistle-stop bling ring fundraiser
wishful-thinking navel gazer
and every inch the sodden downtrodden maverick
it's Reverend Green with the candlestick
mangling the hallowed oesophagus
jangling the keys to your sarcophagus

and all the while seeking fellowship with
an overwatered peace lily and the remnants
of a takeaway rogan josh

Freight train needlepoint ballet dancer
smokescreen querullous fingertip chancer
fragrant polytheistic stylistic mystic
a slash of slut red lipstick
stinging jellyfish tentacles
nettlebed thrumming ventricles

and listening to the strains of Gustav Mahler
it's Miss Scarlett with the revolver
pumping your belly full of lead
until you're deader than the deadest of the dead

and all the while seeking fellowship with
an overwatered peace lily and the remnants
of a takeaway Rogan Josh.

Untitled
by Derek Dohren

There's a sense of fractured timelines
Of souls in the gutter and those in the stars
While chilled fingers feel bony spines
Elon Musk wants us to colonise Mars

There's a stench of managed decay
Of street corner dancers in their overspill
While the plans of billionaires at play
Replace the urban garden windowsill

There's a smell of wanton waste
Of valuable human resource cast aside
While we reach tipping point in undue haste
At the whim and fancy of them inside

There's a swell of myopic treachery
Of bastard figurines cast in fool's gold
While idols in debauched lechery
Ignore all that which can't be sold

**That's Life
by Des Mannay**

Life is shit
Then you die
Ask the question
Wonder why
Here's blood and betrayal
in your eye
God is for sale
with pie in the sky
When love's in your vein
a predictable high
Look in the mirror
your reflection's a lie
Kiss the girls
and watch them fly
Pick yourself up
well, you've got to try
Dust yourself down
Start to cry
Dealing despair
An endless supply
No escape from this pain
no 'right of reply'
Why so polite to my face
when you can't deny
You put the knife in my back
but hate being told that your sly?
So look at the freak
and then decry
Just remember the make up
on which you rely
hides an insecure being
as imperfect as I
Because our lives are like shit
until the day that we die.

A Pearl Amongst Swine
by Des Mannay

Open me up again.
Let me breathe -
let the blood sing in my veins
with the joy of life
and share intimate jokes and looks
that I thought had gone forever,
never to return.
Please do not let
the laughter be a phantom
or your smile be a mirage,
or your very presence
be just a glance
at elegance.
I hold your every word
like jewels
with sweet embellishments
which graze me gently.
Let me bleed happily
and heal with you
the sickness of the past.

Another Day
by Des Mannay

If I seem to slow
It's because I'm not the human dynamo
You used to know

If I start to cry
It's because I can't believe the lie
That's just passed me by

If I seem too free
It's because of what used to be
In the past has meant to me

If I appear down
And sorrow starts to drown
Don't worry - I'll turn around

If I seem all through
Before I look at you
It's what I used to do

If I cannot stay
Before I melt away
I'll be in yesterday

Before you become bound
The future which is found
You'll hear without a sound

Turn over new leaf
Challenge old belief
Feel the relief

Falling from the top
Just like the watch you'll stop
See the body drop.

Faithful
by Dominic Mulgrew

When you're well
I will give you tablets
When you're ill
I will give you bandages
Either way you're a friend
We will get you on the mend
If you're locked away
I will try to visit every day
I will phone you
Not disown you
Look after you on leave
In you I believe
Take you home on day release
Keep you out of trouble with the police
Be there until you're discharged
Have a beer play cards
That's what real mates do
Stay close stay true
Friends until the end
Because I know the real you.

Stressed
by Dominic Mulgrew

Everything seems depressing
Weighed down and stressing
Dark thoughts
Slum resorts
High rise
No surprise
Rubbish ridden
Crime ridden
Benefit fraud
Youngsters bored
Nothing left
Only theft
Money is the root of all evil
Nearly everyone is doing
Something illegal
Going to the food bank
To talk to frank
To citizens advice
To know my rights.

Taking Chances
by Dominic Mulgrew

I get out of bed
Toast some bread
Carefully spread
Take tablets for my head
Pour some tea
Can't take life steadily
Draw my curtains
No certains
Everything's a risk
The wild I miss
But then someone says the wrong word
Calling me absurd
Stealing my bird
I awake at dusk
I hate but I lust
I'm drunk by dawn
I watch porn
Living for my next drink
So out of it I can't think
Doing drugs whatever is on offer
Fighting with an officer
Driving my neighbours mad
Community know I'm bad
Keeping their neighbourhood watch
I'm as cunning as a fox
They want to lock their locks
But I'll show them
I'll knock their locks
I'll shock their docks
I'll rock their quiet drink
And mock society entirely
So I lay in on bed
Burnt my bread
No butter to spread
Skip tablets for my head
Going on a drinking spree

Not taking life steadily
Taking risks
Out in the wild pissed
A bit of an amateur
Not a reformed character.

Could be the Elves
by Donna Meyer
After Paul Simon's "The Werewolf"

In the misty darkness, with the
moon, round and glowing as a doorbell's
chime, the fairies dancing, singing, ringing
around the lawn as if they could
keep evil spirits away, safe as could be,
but in the shadows, something lurks, the
eyes gleam with menace, scattering the elves
the gnomes, the pixies. It is quiet now, but
not a pleasant quiet, for something waits, it's
breathing soft, little grunts, so muted you probably
will not notice them, except now you see the
beast, silhouetted against the moon: the werewolf
- you *think*. You wonder - is that possible? It's
a children's story, a fable, a quarter
of a million years old. Believe if you want to;
I gave all that up when I was twelve.
ah-roo-oo-oo!

(note – This poetic form is called a Golden Shovel, in which the last word of each line forms a line or lines from the original poet's work.)

Ten Thousand Fireflies
by Donna Meyer

Evening
Flying down the highway
There, nestled in a valley
A village
The lights of which are like ten thousand fireflies
who have settled in for the night
Lights of amber and yellow and white
Each light a dinner table
A baby's bath
Dishes being washed
Pajama clad children playing
A quiet conversation
A hundred different acts of daily living
And though this place is unknown to me
It's very name a mystery
My heart whispers the word
"Home."

Bel13ve
by D. S. Scott

It's been thirteen years
But I must believe
There won't be any more
I have no tears to grieve

The life that I once had
It is no longer now
Instead I live like this
And have to wonder how

I've made it through rough times
With so much pain ablaze
Somehow, I stayed alive
Lost in a dreamer's haze

One day it will be over
Just make it through another
Try to stay so strong
When death wants to smother

I'd love to look back some day
And see that I arrived
Maybe there's a promised land
For those who have survived

I'm sure of what I believe in
Positive of what I don't
Quitting isn't an option
And I know that I won't

(Maybe) I Should Forgive Myself
by D. S. Scott

Maybe I should forgive myself
for all the times I was wrong.
Maybe I need to let it slide,
after all, it's been so long.

Maybe I should let it go,
forget about the things I did.
Maybe say goodbye to memories
of what haunted me as a kid.

Maybe I should move on,
give myself some time to feel.
Maybe give the scars time to fade,
let those things in the past heal.

Maybe I should forgive myself
and just maybe regain touch.
Maybe I need to do these things,
but what if that's too much?

Maybe it will be difficult
but it's not like I will die.
Maybe I should forgive myself
or for my own sake, at least try.

Patcher Upper
by Dwane Reads

Are you the patcher upper who I seek to find?
They told me you are patient, gentle, selfless, kind
I am of the broken people. wash me, comb my hair
whisper sweet lullabies softly cradle me to sleep

placate my existence as uncontrollably I weep
for the arms of a loved one I so desperately seek
soothing circled fingers stroke across my crown
rebuilding the broken announce the lost as found

are you the patcher upper who I seek to find?
requesting you to mend me if you'd be so kind
in time I will grow up, be strong, soon become a man
everything not arranged in life try the best you can

I am isolated, unwanted, part broken, beaten, weak
Where is the patcher upper? It's rest bite that I seek
Build me up like Lego transform make me strong
A blue brick to a red brick rebuild me help along

Ignite me like a hot wire. so, sparks mainline a vein
Send purpose in your kind words build me up again
You are the patcher upper who I've been sent to find
Mend me I am broken. Please try, this one last time.

On the Complex
by Dwane Reads

Beyond the outskirts,
stood an empty Victorian asylum.
Where, frequenting demons inside
the heads of tortured minds sang.

Medicated souls made manageable
to a trance like state, by those
compassionless bullies who almost
OD'd on hate, held authority here.

Forgotten bodies, billeted behind
sterile whitewashed brick.
Waiting, like damaged caged birds
frustratingly going nowhere.

Memories, conveniently blank of
the past, hide a disturbed history.
A deliberate stench of underfunding
due to a lack of attention and care.

Landowners invited top developer's
brought in architects, the super-rich
unrecognizable luxury apartments
now offered for sale **on the complex**.

Care in the community now awaits.

Darkness Moves Away
by Eduardo Escalante

Try
cheat
sun
even if it is
a devilment
do not pronounce
words with
the edge of tired lips
appease
pain
with the eyes
of innocence
make fire
for cold instances
not to drown
in what
squeezes
rescue
what is gone
grow fruits
to nourish
the dry fountain
anoint
what does not have
crown
convert
the moon
in a verb
cut
with scissors
nightmares
live
without
the sky dictation

A Different Kind of Glass
by Eduardo Escalante

I spent all morning
trying to draw an orange line in the sky

and fighting not to be
a "copy-paste" of hell,

too much supply of cheap cyanide,
it is like cocaine, the habit will not stop

The human head
keeps seeing twenty seconds late,

impossible a way back. Really pain.
But I try. Like any other good person

when the swamp swallows a herd of lambs,
not only witness. Justice suggests

I have signed the due voice with my own hand
standing by a different shore

away the madness on another side of the window
I intend to keep my stance,

transparent water above all,
someone and somewhere may be lighting

the darkness
— whatever—

forcing a weak tree to tower above a pitch-black foreground.

Before
by Edward Ferrari

Walk when the day
has sharp edges still
and the senses cleave
along the center of the street,
to sun, to shade, and differences
contained; your chest,
opening breath in air
cold enough the smell
comes clean; rosemary,
cut, crushed, and gilded
in gasoline.

After
by Edward Ferrari

I stop at the last set of lights
on the Pkwy and watch
the speed camera
on the other side of the Blvd
go nuts
there are no cars
it reads the light
43, 28, --.

Mind Your Language
by Emerson Wilkes

Born and raised in the Midlands, working Black Country dirt,
By the grace of my Father, old gold is my shirt.
Never asked for a penny, yet taxed for my time,
nose clean and honest, yet fingered for crime.
Raised in an era of 70's glee,
'A thousand apologies' catch-phrased TV.
Now be kind to each other, or you're just no good,
yet our young can't play out cause of rivers of blood.
Proud men in stilettos preparing for prom,
whilst neighbours seek Penthouses to throw them from.

Beautiful girls sat in restaurants, scrolling away,
lip curling 'selfies' they posted that day.
Press that red button, to interact,
called 'device' for a reason, it's time now to act.
Remember your old folks - they lorded their youth,
looking back now I see how they filtered the truth.
Promoting faces to places that shouldn't be there,
bastard caffeine free shampoo, won't grow back my hair.
Mind your language, forty-something or you'll cause a row,
I'm off for my favourite curry, so Ciao x

Tonight
by Faleeha Hassan

When I entered my apartment
The stairs were lying like tired men after a hard day's work
The door a yawning mouth
My TV was listening intently to the sports newscast
And
Like a huge fat woman, the couch was sitting on the floor
Hardly breathing the used air
The curtain tickled the cheek of the window……..
Swaying gracefully above
My books slept like babies on the hands of the bookshelves
The dining table was listening to the whispers of her chairs
The lamps were winking at to each other
The fan was busy flailing her arms indifferent
In my apartment
The life looks the same as I left it
Everything is normal
No,
It is more than normal
Strang…….
No one missed me?

Empty Poem
by Faleeha Hassan

Let me address everyone here in the third person
I will call the friend who quickly left my life with all this mess
and never cleaned it up...
"he"
And I will call the man who continues gently knocking on the door
of my heart every moment
and I smile at him...
"he"
I will describe the bird
his wing collided yesterday with the glass of my car
and I cried...
"he"
And I will point to the man
I see him now jogging in his shorts with all this snow
and I shivering ....
"he"
And I will name the dog
who barks angrily whenever I walk on this street
" he"
And you will be guessing what I meant in each section
For example, when I say,
"he" was flying a plane so low
I did not notice his flight
That does not mean I'm talking about the dog
If I say, "he" did not care about all those snow piles
I certainly did not mean by that
That the friend who left behind him the smoke of gossip and the
fire of tears and some poems
After I finish this poem I will send it to a hard-working critic
He publishes daily his work in all the magazines
And like a strong-faith woman I will sit
Praying with patience
Yes
these days
a poem does not need a subject in order to be written
and to become important

It seems
I don't actually need to be a poet to be invited to a poetry festival.

I Ask You
by Gail Moran Slater

To create the sensibility by which I'm understood,
the way the Earth senses a new season,
I imagine knowing it before.
When did I know it before?
You say we have known it all along.

If at last I wander past the lament of the surf
into realms of pure beauty and kindness, I ask you,
what would that look like?

You walk ahead of me. I've been pursuing you
to ask about all this, and now that I am near,
you have nothing to say.

We have wandered into a place of pure beauty and kindness,
together, you say. We are unfettered, you say.
Isn't that enough?

100 Words
by Gail Moran Slater

Winter Earth slogs toward the light,
mid-March unloads icicles from trees,
slackens strident winds.
The stern sea relaxes into my gaze--
six years old, waiting on the waterside
before Daddy calls come in. I'm yearning
for a time, I've not known
though I know who I am.

So many times, before,
so many times, to come,
I have strained to create a form
by which I am understood.
I need discipline. I need a compass
and straight edges.
How do I know such things at six?
The way the Earth senses a new season.

You
by Geoff Bennett

This is for you.
Picked and plucked and placed for you.

Taut and tight and right and fit.

Feel it vibrate in your ears,
In your eyes, your tears.

Let go your fears.

Immerse your mind
Deep in its sound.

What have you found?

Speak. Seek. See.
Be free.

That thought you've caught,

It's yours.
It's new.
It's beautiful.

It's you.

Worthy Burden
by Geoff Bennett

This load! . . . . .
She struggled on,
Through days beset with cold
And each jerked step away from bed
Wrenched hip and back and teared her eyes.
Those life-long days December bled.
Her struggled breath and shuddered sighs.
She felt so very old.

Why should life bring so much pain?
Without pain there is no gain,
Says the athlete with each pant.
A glib, unphilosophical rant.

Existence stands before a fall.
A weary care, yet clear to all
Who live and lived. What more to say?
Her torment stopped one brilliant day.

An end? . . . . .
Her struggle gone,
At least an end to strain.
Such surge of joy surpassing all,
For there beside her soaking head,
The sweetest reason for it all,
Surprised, eyes wide, skin soft and red.
New life. Her child. Their gain.

The Things I Wished I Didn't Do
by Gerald Kells

The things I wished I didn't do
started with one and went to two,
soon were four and five and six,
they made a tower of vapid bricks,
slight and tall it reached to ten
and then a hundred and, then again,
a million bricks, a tower completed,
the things I might do lay defeated.

Wretched Poet
by Gerald Kells

Wretched poet,
say something nice,
I would value
good advice.

But all your verse
is dreary cant,
your inadequacy
both sad and scant -

Oh, make me laugh,
please, poet, do
or what's the bloody
use in you?

Synthesis
by Ian Davies

I used to think
If I chose not live
How much would I be missed?

This thought tormented me
For so many years as I walked
Wrapped in my cloak of vain glory

Until, emotionally, I died
I ceased to be and life carried on
Oblivious to my suffering

Until I sparked,
What was this spark?
A simple snowflake

A transient speck of frozen water
How did this inconsequential entity
Have the power to jolt my soul

From my self-imposed purgatory
I realised how wrong I had become
I did not bring meaning to life

I was not the pivot
On which all things turn
I was transient like the snowflake

I realised there was so much I was not seeing
Not feeling in my introverted world
I realised life would go on

Every sunrise bringing vigour and warmth
Golden tipped leaves falling in autumn
The first frost of winter painting patterns on windows

Spring bringing promise of regeneration
The musky breathe of summer
The turning of the seasons

Smiles of joy and sorrow
The tingling touch of intimacy
All this would continue

Life would continue
In all it's confusing, painful,
Frustrating, joyous glory

Now in quieter times
I think if I had chosen to die
How much I would have missed

The Final Performance of the Great Ridiculous Hermaphrodite
by Ian Davies

Roll up!
Roll up!
Roll up!
Ladies and Gentlemen
Mothers and children
The greatest spectacle known to man
The Great Ridiculous Hermaphrodite
Is giving its final performance

Roll up!
Roll up!
Roll up!
More woman than man
More dead than alive
The Great Ridiculous Hermaphrodite
Never to be seen again
A wonder not to be missed

Take your seats
And be amazed as it performs
Its non-abusive self-flagellation
Watch closely as the stains
Are reabsorbed
To leave not one trace of damage inflicted

See it perform its cranial contortions
Twisting its brain again and again
Until backwards is forwards
And upside is down

Sit aghast as The Great Ridiculous Hermaphrodite
Attempts to submerge itself
In a vat of its own shit
Not for 30 seconds
Not for 30 minutes

But for 30 years
Without once surfacing for air

Thrill as The Great Ridiculous Hermaphrodite
Hangs by its balls 1000 feet above ground
Attempting to untie its knots
Without aid of a safety net
To plummet into a thimbleful of pity

But rest assured folks
If the spectacle gets too much
If its suffering becomes unbearable
Remember all you are witnessing
Is accomplished by deft application
Of reflective surfaces and mist
So roll up!
Roll up!
Roll up!
Don't miss this once in a lifetime opportunity
Just leave your baggage at the entrance
Cos the show is about to begin
And it is performing just for you

**Now and Then I Have to Come Face to Face
by Ian Davies**

The difference
Between me and you
Is three and two
The moon sees true
My carcass ridden zoo
Where who is who
No time to stare
Can't leave it there
Its killing me I swear
Laying me bare
Stranded and naked
Trying to fake it
Don't think I'll make it
Just end up deflated
When I feel I should be
Congratulated
And differences
Keep showing through
Can't seem to be enough for you
Don't see the gate I'm passing through
Can't find the path
I wish they wouldn't laugh
A cross on a graph
Nailed to a bloodied lath
Sinking and floating
Breathing and choking
Beating then stroking
"Keep the flow
Soon it will go"
How long?
"I don't know"
Just waiting for the glow
Finding that golden bow
To shoot my arrow into the sun
To lift me when I run
And rest my head

When day is done
Where I cradle my soul
When fears and self-loathing
Become too much for my body to take.

At the Window
by Ian Henery

At the window, waiting for your return,
This sad face is reflected in cracked pane
And at my lonely post I will remain.
My candle, for you, shall forever burn,
Your beautiful smile and laughter, I yearn;
My life a shade under the pale moonlight,
Sleepless eyes and pale flesh in the day light,
Logic and rational thought I have spurned.

So, tell me - am I wasting my time?
A custodian of just broken dreams,
promises broken, shattered at the seams?
Judged, tried and sentenced - but what was my crime?
This longing is an agony sublime,
A sweet melancholy of cruel heart break,
Haunting me all the hours I am awake,
My disposition told to you in rhyme.

Black Country Water
by Ian Henery

The swag by the new housing estate
Is littered with used up disposables,
Refuse from a TV-fed population,
Making their home by a water-filled quarry.
Damp cardboard, rotting prams and bin liners
Mark their final passage, their journey`s end.

In the gaps between traffic and house work
Children climb between railings and keep out signs
Fishing for frogs, toasters and shopping trolleys,
Small human beings drawn to the water,
Rippling in the moonlight, lapping under the stars,
Primeval swamp of humanity`s birth.

Water - it's mind calls to us from the drains,
Gutters and swimming pools across brick houses
As we watch TV and washing machine cycles.
The holy font of water is like a universe
In this utopia of ice cream vans and job centres,
A water siren calling us all back home.

Above the swag, stars blister in an icy sky
And Atlantic waves echo in the water,
Rustling through stunted thickets at its edge,
Crashing heads against broken bricks and marl clay.
A petrol sheen on the swag mirrors the moon,
Dark clouds reflected in the still dark water.

Liar
by J Snow

All [my] life,
I prided [my]self for being honest.

then [my] 'ol man looked down the barrel of a 9mm pistol one morning at 6:11,
decided HE wanted to taste copper, and swallowed a bullet,
and HE did it for [me],
an intentional, profound, purposeful punish[me]nt

I know HIS last thought was in the shape of a wish —
hatred s[me]ared onto [me] by [my] son, and HIS,
blisters on [my] heart,
for HE believed [my] own son would turn away from [me] like HIS father turned away from HIM
when HE was of the sa[me] age as ours,
just a baby of six,
believing deep in the withered recesses of HIS black, cold heart
HIS family would teach HIM to ham[me]r [my] spirit into splinters,
and HE was right —
they did try
because they needed so[me]one to bla[me]
other than themselves

HE prayed strong to a god HE couldn't bring to mind,
regardless the hours of scripture study,
to make [me] feel as HE felt when HE pulled the trigger
for no other reason than HE believed I, a liar, was cheating on HIM
when I drove ho[me] to visit [my] family in Virginia like I did every sum[me]r,
as if that being \true\ would excuse HIS action of licking cold steel at a forty degree angle,
a [me]ans to send our son
straight into the fla[me]s of a hell he created

HIS mother lays bla[me] on [my] lap with smiles and winks,
and I realize grief s[me]lls like whiskey and weed
and looks like dry, cracked lips caked with white at the corners,
giggly and childish in the depths of denial

all [my] life,
I prided [my]self for being honest

she nursed her own son with a bottle of liquor,
then taught HIM how to roll a joint when reality beca[me] too hard to hold on to,
'Just run and run and don't worry, no news is good news, go have you so[me] fun,
but don't let your step-dad know,
never tell HIM a thing!'
HIS mother taught HIM to lie,
and they both lied, even to each other,
denying lie after lie with another lie upon lie until the day HE died,
and that's when I took HIS place as the liar beside her

I wonder if she'd instead taught HIM to be kind and strong and confident,
to take a deep breath and count down from ten when rage took control,
if maybe HE would've found a frag[me]nt of peace in HIS life
and not fought so hard to destroy all peace in [mine]

maybe

I used to wonder if she had taught HIM to respect HIMself and others ,
wo[me]n in particular,
if HE'd still have beaten [me] down physically, [me]ntally,
but ignorant I was to think such a way
when respect is a thing she herself is unable to be taught,
but lies about it anyway
with a yellowing, jagged, toothy smile plastered on her face

she made a liar out of HIM,
and that was all,
then HE,
a liar out of [me]

I lie and tell her she did nothing wrong,
that she had no choice but to emotionally destroy her own son
to please the man that ca[me] into her life to "save" them from
starvation and certain ho[me]lessness,
a provider, trading the life of her first born for a house and a
na[me],
and I tell her she's not to bla[me],
choking back vomit as the words fall from [my] mouth

I lie with nods of agree[me]nt and act like her advice is solid and
sound,
as though she never made a mistake in her life
as she ducks around the corner to down another shot and smoke a
little weed,
and I recall false [me]mories to make her feel the warmth of
nostalgia,
and all she ever wants in return is to destroy [me]
because I chose life,
but her son chose death

I hold secret the ti[me] HE told [me] HE hated HIS mother
or when HE said,
'she only comes to get high. she doesn't give a fuck about me, and
I don't give a fuck about her.
I don't think she wants to be my mother.
I don't think she ever loved me,'
but HE said it with no emotion,
like a passing thought,
though HE [me]ant every word of it,
and it's the one thing I'm sure HE didn't lie about

I don't tell her the other things HE said too,
even when she keeps shoving [my] head under water,

and I am torn, unsure what to do —
I should tell her because maybe she'd swallow a bullet too
and do [me] the sa[me] favor HE did;
I shouldn't because [my] baby boy of six can't handle any
more death

I want to tell her but can't,
though the words churn in [my] guts and feel like a fire was lit
in the center of [me],
burning at the edges
and then I realize I'm holding [my] breath,
imagining the rat clawing at [my] insides trying to chew
HIMself out,
and that's a lie by omission,
but it's a lie all the sa[me]
just like her hiding the fact she drove [my] son ho[me] while
stoned stupid,
and I lie by not telling her I know
because I know she will lie right back to [me],
incapable of owning up to any-damn-thing

But, how do you explain to a mother no one could love her
son,
a narcissistic sociopath who chose death as a way to punish
another
not HIMself,
and how do you tell your own son,
and HIS,
what HE really was in life?

you don't

you lie

And, how do you tell the sister HE hated they you wish her no
harm
after she's harassed and stalked you since HIS death,
desperate not to see \truth\,
creating a victim of herself alone

and I, the villain of her story

You don't lie

the \truth\ is too painful and justifiable to keep as your own

Now, both HIS mother and sister want [my] son as their own,
but deny it, lie about it,
thinking (him) a second chance
like mother might get it right this ti[me]
and sister won't miss so much ti[me] by HIS side,
thinking it'll erase the mistakes that were made,
the time that was unused given back again,
so they question [my] parenting decisions
though I choose to not teach [my] own to drink away troubles or smoke to hide pain
or give (him) a reason to feel a need to either for the sake of happiness

I don't lie about that

I never lie about that

the man who looked down the barrel of a 9mm pistol
and decided no one in HIS life hurt near enough for HIS taste
was dead long before HE pulled the trigger,
and I will always lie,
not to save them from pain because I do want them to hurt, want them to burn,
but because I fear it will take from [my] son (his) last breath of hope the world isn't shit
because (he) still bla[me]s (him) self,
even when I tell (him) only daddy is to bla[me]

that's not a lie

I lie to (him) of other things though,
to comfort (his) tears,
and I lie to [my]self that I'm protecting (him) by lying and lying,

but the \truth\ is
they are slowly turning (him) into (his) father,
and I'm terrified I will open (his) bedroom door in a few years
and find only pieces of (him),
having lied to [my]self that I could stop this train running wild
without brakes
all over the tracks and headed for [me] with (him) in the seat,
but still I can't stop lying because I lie mostly to [me]

I lie and I lie and I lie to [my] son
and tell (him) (his) daddy was a good man, a great man, a
strong and smart man
who loved (him) above all others
and never wanted to hurt (him),
and I will lie to (him) forever
because I don't want (him) to know half of (him) ca[me] from
a coward
worth nothing in life and even less in HIS death,
nothing but a liar

the \truth\ is
[he] alone pulled the trigger
and no other can claim blame or pass it from one to another
[he] was frail and weak as [he] always called ME
and what I lie about, and fear is the \truth\
is I was or am or will be as selfish and worthless as [he].

Nothing
by J Snow

Nothing is quite as striking
As trauma chiseled into a face

Nothing is quite as horrific
As the thoughts that I embrace

Nothing is quite as painful
As a mind falling from grace

Nothing is quite as breathtaking
As the freedom that I chase

Barricade
by J Snow

You breathed life into my spirit
then set it on fire
stomped it into nihility again

Agony expands its jagged-toothed maw
grief spreads serrated talons
their glares as untamed flame
despair yawns before me like a cavernous wound

Trepidation stitches a barricade around me
its stone riddled with cracks
its tiny window warped with age

I Chose You
by J. L. Lane

When it felt like the world was closing in on me,
Like I lost all that I used to be,
When it felt like I couldn't take anymore,
Like I was going to collapse to the floor,
I chose you.

When my eyes filled up with tears,
and my soul filled up with fears,
When I felt like my insides were filled with screams,
And nightmares hijacked my dreams,
I chose you.

When my memories caused me too much pain,
or I found myself crying yet again,
When I sat alone at night,
And darkness extinguished my light,
I chose you.

When everything about me felt wrong,
and I felt that I just couldn't be strong,
When I stared at my own reflection,
And all I felt was rejection,
I chose you.

Hiding away in my drawer you sat,
Under a pile of clothes you lay flat.
Shimmering as I exposed your sharpness,
Always there in my moments of darkness,
I chose you.

Piercing my flesh with ease,
Never caring about my families pleas,
releasing the crimson from my arm,
There to serve one purpose; to harm,
I chose you.

Now I wear my scars with shame,
with only myself here to blame,
They fade but never leave me alone,
and now that my soul has finally grown,
I regret that I chose you.

All-Day Suckers
by James Michael Shoberg

One little leech sensed Gordon splashing blithely in the bog.
A second little leech appeared from underneath a log.
A third, having completed its cocoon of tiny eggs,
Accompanied the second on the backs of Gordon's legs.
A fourth went forth to his right foot and sipped a tasty toe.
Five, six, and seven followed suit to drink the pedal flow.
Next eight (who hadn't eaten) came, quite ravenous to dine,
And fixed itself upon a thigh by thirsty number nine.
 Alas, ten and eleven found they had to deeper delve,
Because the patch they wanted had been seized by number twelve.
The thirteenth in succession was the first to claim a cheek,
One under Gordon's swimming trunks—the parasitic sneak.
But Gordon was oblivious, though he grew chilled and numb,
To tingles that had heralded the hundreds yet to come.
And just below the surface—not that one should be surprised—
His legs had turned a slimy black with suckers that incised.
"It sure is cold for summer," Gordon thought while turning pale,
Unconscious of the frenzy hidden by the cloudy veil.
"Perhaps it's time to call it quits; I've swum about since noon.

The light of day is fading and my skin is like a prune."
So Gordon plodded toward the grass which framed the misty marsh,
And pondered why this simple task was strenuous and harsh.
Then, through a haze, his eyes took in the horror with a glance:
He saw a "swamp tuxedo"—stark white shirt and ebon pants,
Except the pants were pulsing as they drank his youthful blood.
The shock of it had sent him reeling back into the mud.
He sank down in the water, fully feeling the effect,
While waves of darting leeches sought out places to connect.

And there, exsanguinated, he is drowning in the murk,
Which is my cue to join the rest and set my teeth to work.
I like my meals immobile; now, the boy can hardly slog,
And that's why I've been waiting since I sensed him in the bog.

False Tooth
by James Michael Shoberg

Nightmares quite scary had often plagued Carrie, who dreamed that her teeth all fell out.
She struggled to bury those thoughts, which grew hairy, but still she'd awake with a shout.
In sleep, she was wary, and she'd have to parry a rather odd creature she saw:
Its eyes, small and glary, would focus on Carrie, expressly what fell from her maw.
So she did not tarry, that wily girl Carrie, to formulate one of her schemes—
Determined that nary one tooth it would ferry away from her mouth in those dreams.
And luckily, Mary, the sister of Carrie, had just lost a loose pearly white—
She'd never think Carrie with fingers most airy would pilfer her molar one night.
But on the contrary, the sly, thieving Carrie, in fear of the visions she had,
Believed her primary concern should be Carrie and not, "What if Mary gets mad?"
Committed to vary those nightmares quite scary, she slipped the tooth under her head—
The tooth of poor Mary, repurposed by Carrie, to sate what would visit her bed.
You see, clever Carrie knew her adversary, that is to say, she had a hunch—
"A thing legendary," supposed the young Carrie, "Which gathers what we use to munch."
With confidence, Carrie became sedentary, and drifted off into repose.
Her fantasies merry, she saw nothing scary; well, not until morning's light rose.
For red as a cherry, fresh blood leaked from Carrie, her mouth full of sockets and sores—
And that's because Carrie had crossed the Tooth Fairy, who knows when a tooth is not yours.

Tired
by James Michael Shoberg

She moves only inches—the dear little lump.
Each time she's disturbed, she will shift again—*bump*.
Her rosy red dress has grown soiled with mud.
That must be from playing—well, most of it—*thud*.
And there's her sweet dolly, not far from her reach.
I wonder what name she had given it—*screech*.
She rolls as if waking, now turned on her back.
Her lids remain closed, for she's not been roused—*crack*.
I'd go to her, surely, but no cars have slowed,
And what good are two of us dead in the road?

A Birdless Cage
by Jason Conway

I keep my pets hungry
trapped in my mind
a cage left unrattled
my monsters are fine
they growl at my pain
like acid
stripping atrophy
bones clean
raw from the fray
daily doubt
gnaws at my gates
rusting with each attack
torrents of insecurity
relentless
unhindered
narcotic

For I am consumed
by fire and stone brimmed
rivers of lava
devour all that's good
leaving red and black
from the beasts attack
evil and sorrow
fear and sleep
shadows to reap

I am broken
cracked
blacked
a fading token
of self
as blood runs open
wounds unspoken
hidden from view
and kept locked

in Jones' locker
under crushing seas
of unease

The black sister teases
a shouldered muse
whispering wired barbs
that rip without mercy
heresy
to believe I was free
from the other me
the one that cowers
dreamless
cold
and hollow

Dark rages
blind fury's
thrashing
indiscriminate
peeling away pages
leathered words
burned with hot irons
under tarnished skin
unforgiven

An oilless man of tin
seized
bled
empty of hope
an unlit candle
lost
security tossed
aside
left to fester
as the rot spreads

Time is still
brain lies ill

poisoned by pills
of bitterness
regrets
joy to forget
walls crumble
tombs unearthed
quaking
taking
my will
like a wolf to a flock
thoughts amok
racing for weakness
searching for unturned proof
riddles unwritten
by the gods
stricken
in my glass prison
a birdless cage
with nowhere to hide

Bleak futures spied
hope to deride
before I wake
to gaze at futures mirror
to seek but a smile
a grain of empathy
as the grass of envy
blankets
the fortunes of others
for love is theirs
hope in pairs

Dry tears
ghost empty ducts
dust settled
on opportunity
like a keyless lock
shackled
restrained

subservient
to a spiralling master
dreams to shatter
shards to pitter
and patter
like fallen stars
yet to find a home

I keep my pets hungry
till my new face is found

Shipwrecked
by Jason Conway

Baneful claws infect
Ending restful sleep for sweat
Augmented horrors
Scratching slumbered hope-filled doors
Terrified dreams sink shipwrecked

Wonderment frozen
Ailing heart trembling laid bare
Lone crew abandoned
Killed by salted beasts of doom
Silenced soul mourned by full moon

Nighted steeds trample
Innocent dreams left unborn
Gales whip a beached hull
Howling banshee of remorse
Tugs my windless sails apart

Moored in raw tempest
Alone in naked despair
Revenant awakes
Elysium fields burning
Sleep bequeathed to raging sea

Terrified dreams sink shipwrecked
Sleep bequeathed to raging sea
fearful tears bloodstain the decks
haunted by the ghosts of me.

Beach of My Soul
by Jason N Smith

The sound of waves washing over senses
serenading our once turbulent thoughts
soothing with lullabying lapping waves
disengaging cares with peaceful songs,

and I could lay here for all of eternity
beneath these tall green vibrant trees
leaves dancing jigs within a breeze and
celebrating summer warmth outwards

to the waves lapping upon the beach
as two lovers kiss before slow retreat
beseeching feet to wonder onto wet
sand once left, but we never forget

grit between toes and rippling moon
shimmering a distant dance and hue
long past all of our journeys' home
into memories reverie until a new...

Darkness is a Womb
by Jason N Smith

Inside darkness,
a terrifying and dread filled darkness.
A darkness where we fear raising our voices,
a darkness fearing echoing reverberations
of footfalls raising up a dust
and a predatory hunters hunger descending
to disseminate and dismember paths,
paths paced along the banks of Babylon and down,
down to and into and out of ages past
and emerging today,
A today where we discover,
where we discover that this darkness,
that this terrible darkness is a blessed womb birthing life,
A beautiful and most precious life,
where our voices are birthed and become shouts of jubilant joy
Where people dance exuberant on whispered revolutionary words
and every single utterance is heard
and there is life.
A life where glorious abundance flows umbilical
before births beginning back beyond waters broken,
where we are thrust forth, poured forth from heavenly homes,
we are birthed,
we are birthed as a the darkness hovers over faces of our deeps
birthed out of nurturing wombs we believed were our tombs
but we are just incubated embryotic buoyant bubbles during interludes,
before being birthed out of our darkness.

Can You Hear us Calling?
by Jason N Smith

Are you listening?

Then listen to clambering calls from WE
that once lived
resonating resounding sound in one voice:
Value every breath that you have left
and do not dwell on our deaths,
for we do not cry it's cold and dark here,
we do not call for blame in our names,
nor for patterns repeating once again,
we sing out songs of eternal peace
seeking collective unity,

in YOUR commiserations.
Are you listening?

Believe in Self Belief
by Jan Hedger

Take a risk and leave the shadows
With vibrant clothes that sing out loud
Be yourself in rhythmic echoes
Emerge with strength, discard the shroud.

Draw your breath as the music grows
Play your cards, to the captive crowd
Take a risk and leave the shadows
With vibrant clothes that sing out loud.

Hail! The gift of melodic vows
With which we are richly endowed
Blow the whistle silvery proud
Hear the applause, embrace the bows
Take a risk and leave the shadows
With vibrant clothes that sing out loud.

Been a Poor Year
by Jan Hedger

Unripe acorns crunch under booted
feet treading the towpath; a
carpet of brokenness
of winter fodder.

Some fall into dark water
of Llangollen Canal.
Plops, spasmodic, more resonant
than silent raindrops, create
single rippled circles, spreading
outwards to a wider circumference, on
coal black surface.

Acorns sink into thick
silted mud, no value in
nutrition.

Knife
by Jean Aked

Sharp
Edges
Cutting deep
Into my heart,
Bringing us to the place where we must part.

Slumber
by Jean Aked

Sweet slumber
That brings thoughts of you
To my mind,
Releasing
From the routine and dull grind
Each day brings to me.

Waffling
by Jean Aked

Writing poetry together,
Always with the theme of love,
For we are as one together
Flying free on wings of love;
Loving as we have never loved—
In each other's arms we linger,
Now and always
Growing closer.

Have You Ever Felt
by Jennie Baron

Have you ever felt
On the edge of life but not quite part of it?
Like happiness is at your fingertips
But just beyond your grasp?
Have you ever felt
That you were looking in
 From a cold night
Through a lighted window
At a warm room
Where smiling people
Share a meal and a drink,
Music and affectionate companionship?
That maybe you could go inside,
Be a part of it,
If only you had the courage
To ring the damn doorbell?
Have you ever felt like a child
In a world full of grownups
All beautiful and accomplished,
Intelligent and articulate?
That anything you have to say
Is so elementary to them?
That to them inevitably
You are only a child?
An orphaned child
Who never has and never will know
The love and warmth of family?
Have you wondered how much
 You'll ever truly matter to another?
How much you can accomplish in life?
If you understand what I say,
 You know how easy it is to despair.
 You learn to function despite those demons
 You and I share.
 You keep a stiff upper lip.
 You carry on, but they're always there.

The darkness resurfaces now and then
And you don't even know why.
I wish I could meet and talk with you
And together we could keep them at bay.
If you don't understand,
And I hope you never do,
Sympathize and be kind because
You never know what lies
Deep beneath the surface
Of those you encounter on any ordinary day.

Luminous
by Jennie Baron

Your eyes are the Fourth of July
Your smile the light of day
But the light in your heart
Is much brighter by far
And it leaves me dazed
And completely amazed
Just to glimpse one tiny ray.

You're luminescent, incandescent, brilliantly bright
But I know all about the fire behind the light
Let me warm myself beside it
Always want to reignite it
Light my way and stay within my sight.

When the Lord said, "Let there be light,"
He had you in mind for me.

A constellation, no doubt
With my own North Star.

Your glow defined
The dark corners of my mind
And set my spirit free.

Within These Red Walls
by Jozilea Faulkner

One Friday night
Walking home
One empty girl
All alone

Between the light
There's nothing but dark
Her twisting hair
Her beating heart

"There's nothing there
Nothing to fear
You're being stupid
There's nobody there"

She repeats that verse
Again, and again
Trying to convince
That she is sane

The silence creeps
Calling from the shadow
Screaming at her
From every hallow

She digs deep
Trying to find
Her music & peace
Her way to hide

Her way to hide
From the Darkness and cold
To even her breath
Her body, her soul

"There's nothing there

Nothing to fear
You're being stupid
There's nobody there"

The music breaking
The silence like ice
Her heart not slowing
Her face going white

"There's something there
I can feel it inside
Nowhere to run
Nowhere to hide..."

She looks behind
Over her shoulder
And just as she'd said
There was nobody there

But she was so sure
Of her feeling so deep
She tried not to look
She tried not to weep

Half way there
To the safety and warm
To her sister and niece
And her bedroom, her home

A hand on her shoulder
The same as before
She had seen nothing
She was so sure...

He pulled her back
He dragged her down
She was going under
She started to drown

A dove glided down
Watching the scene
Of the broken teen
Too scared to scream

The shadow grew
And swallowed her whole
Couldn't see street lamps
Her vision it stole

She was under
Her body was limp
Into the car
That he stuffed her in

Between those lights
In nothing but black
Perfect for cover
Perfect for an attack

She opened her eyes
Struggled to see
Past the cloud of her eyes
And the dusty debris
In a room
Somewhere unknown
Tied to a beam
Again alone

She couldn't scream
She couldn't cry
She couldn't feel
She didn't know why

She didn't know where
She didn't know how
She bowed her head
Looking to the ground

There was something there
Paper in print
She thought it was her name
but she had to squint

It was so dark
With a dim light
This was her prison
The end of her life

She dragged the paper
with her bare feet
To see the writing
On this one sheet

That one sheet
held her destiny to come
this person knew her
And he was having fun

You opened your mouth
When silence was asked
Now I give you
The silence you lack

You've stolen my life
Now I steal yours
No more family
No more outdoors

You shouldn't have told
Now my prison I face
You chose mine
So, I chose your fate

It was all your fault
From the very start
Your accusations so clear;
They broke my heart

So, it's obsession or love?
That I'm not sure
Now stay trapped forever
within these red walls

Finally, it hit her
His familiar eyes
The one that had fed her
All those sickening lies

He's not done it once
But now he's done it twice
Broken her heart
Stolen her life

"There's nothing there
But everything to fear
You weren't being stupid
But now nobody's there"

Find Inspiration in Emptiness
by Jozilea Faulkner

If we could see the future,
where would we be today?
Too scared to let people loves us,
because we know how we'd be betrayed?
Consumed by searching for a painless road,
only to find that, one doesn't exist.
Becoming stuck in limbo,
because you couldn't put yourself through it.
You'd miss out on all the laughter,
the love, the life,
the tears.
All for the sake of finding some kind of faultless experience?
Our society has become obsessed with perfection.
Sharing only the parts of our lives that we deem worthy,
anything less is seen as weakness.
But why?
Life is more than the good times.
It's the broken hearts, the lessons learned the hard way.
All of those things made you who you are today.
So, love the wrong person,
say the wrong things.
Eat until you feel sick.
Declare your passionate feelings.
Wear something that will make you look back and cringe.

Stop trying to be perfect.
Nobody is.

Every Ghost Will Return
by Jude Brigley

Time closes in once more
and reminds her that spaces
between then and now
are only a moon's eclipse.

She wonders if the wounds
that opened up sorrows
still long to mouth their words
like greedy carnivores.

How can fortune
still hold her in a grip
under the vacuum of sky
that sucks out dark birds?

Bound in the binaries
of feather and claw
she has learnt
that this too will pass.

But, tonight she feels her body
in the expanse where all
locate themselves,
lost with indifferent things,
lost to the meanings she makes.

Exfiltration
by Jude Brigley

Standing at the top of the dark hill,
the descent whispered with a mouth of hell.

It was his mind that opened like a wound
and flagrantly sucked the beating heart.

Rather than face the man he had become
he walked the road to miss the park

where through the railings hands might
pull his coat and leave him undisguised.

Treading the pavement with a tawny cat,
his watchfulness startled beneath street lights.

Hints of silent footfall on the path,
And bushes in a dudgeon at being edged,

to avoid the insistence of torn thorns
which might face him with himself.

Black Dog
by James WF Roberts

It wraps around me
like a blanket on a winter's night
the horrendous old familiar
that warm emptiness.

I feel behind my eyes
the longing to cry
the burning, that never goes
away.

I can't get out of bed
world's all spinning
jumbled up inside my head
I'm exhausted before I make the door
I'd cry myself to sleep
but the tears would never stop.

Why—when everyone's happy
I am so miserable?
'happy birthday to you'…they're all singing
I'm in the middle of the room like an offering
to a narcissistic god.

But, how would it feel
to not breathe again?
How would it feel
to have never existed at all?
another needle in the vein
another joyful, burning,
imbedded blade.

'you must take your meds.
'you must take your meds.
they will make you better…'
then why do they make me worse?
'it's just body getting used to them…'

The voices in my head
never, ever, ever end
is this my house
or a hall of mirrors
I'm drowning in a sea
of accusatory stares
everyone I pass
On the street

I know they're looking at me
I know they all hate me
I know they're all judging me

No matter what I say
no matter I do
I can't ever beat this blue
what would it matter
if tomorrow I never woke
up at all?
who would care
if I never existed at all?

No matter what I do
he's always on my tail,
I can hear him breathing
in the hall way.
Black dog's sniffing,
scratching at my door again…

Do You?
by James WF Roberts

Do you remember
our first night—together alone?
you lying naked on the bed,
your body glowing in the moonlight
your wedding ring, on a chain around
your neck, dangling dormant
in the valley of your breasts?
Moonlit shadows,
half-closed venetians
cutting a noir-ish blue
across this secret room…
What joys
what infinite delights
did we share?
first time bliss
was not just another word
in the dictionary
first time bliss
wasn't just another
few hundred of white
you've injected in your arm.
Reading you Sartre
you reading me Marvel comics
bodies entwined as we argue
existence of love, of G-d
the existence of non-existence
the non-existence of existence
If only we had those nights again
before our war of blood
and hate—before you broke
into my flat; to prove
I wasn't alone
before the court dates
and our friends taking sides

Only speaking once
for the first time in 4 years
and you remind me of my feelings
for you and your control of me
by hearing you on the end of the line…

Going back into our old conversations,
telling me how much you missed me
how much you remember me…'all the time'.
Joyless years of drink
drugs and sex
of trying to find
those nights again
with anyone who'll take me
final finding love again
but me destroying it
because she now reminds
me too much of you…
If only those nights still remained?

Brooklyn Soothsayer
by Judy Shepps Battle

The prophet's tale was preordained
told by a wise lady
magic ball in wizened hand
voice creaking with horror.

She told how life would begin anew
stretch into a furlong of Hell
stink of stale desire
muted by impossibility and
drenched in hostility.

Ears covered, eyes shut
we ran to nowhere
rested everywhere
cursing the rising fear and
choking on the putrid odor.

In the distance, quite near really
the hoary voice moaned possessed
begging to be believed.

Stone Archway
by Karen Horsley

Standing under a stone archway
my feet bathe in a puddle of rain
water drips from wringing clothes
runs down bare legs, adding depth
to the pond beneath my toes
The tunnel stretches in front of me
no distant horizon welcoming
as light absorbed by darkness
cold air pulses on my wet skin
a shiver runs down my spine
A glance behind reassuring me
there's no way back, no return
the life I leave is no longer mine
the rain comes down steadily
washing away all memories
The only choice to step forward
into the tunnel, into uncertainty
of what this dark future holds
blank as my unseeing eyes
bleak as the echo calling me.

White Light Shadow
by Karen Horsley

Lost in the shadows of my mind
Thoughts break like waves
And retreat
Pulling a part of me with them
Sand and pebbles dragged under water
Clouding my thoughts, suspended particles
Swirl furiously, then settle
Residual fog persists within
My mind, the ocean

Close my eyes, listen to the waves
Determination building
They crash
My mind, the shoreline
Strewn with flotsam
Twinkling treasure catches my eye
Shrouded by broken promises
The wreckage of life
Draws you down

Dark deep waters, no glimmer of light
Lifeless, stagnant
Silence falls, hope fades
Floating, sinking
Into the abyss
The fissures in your mind
A chasm of lost dreams
Shadows shield
Your bright, white light.

For Z and L
by Kathryn Carter

Baby blue eyes go to sleep,
So, you can't see your mother weep,
She cradles you softly, wrapped in lace,
And whispers "you were too perfect for this place".

A tear rolls down her rosy cheeks,
She had carried you safely for weeks and weeks,
She gave you life from within herself,
If only she could have given you health.

The anger, the sadness, the blame,
Everyone is sorry and it's "such a shame",
She wanders through her life in such a cloud,
and even the silence seems so loud.

But someone had chosen you for much more special things,
And with your new found halo you also got your wings,
So, you could fly between two places,
and see your mummies "happy faces"
whenever she looked back on your birth,
and remembered that you were once on earth,
and you were so loved, she tells you this,
Whilst she's giving your pictures a little kiss,
and stroking the hand print that she only got to touch,
and then again, she whispers "I miss you very much"
So, you can know she's ok and rest within her heart,
Because although you are in heaven, you never are apart.

And She Just Sang/Caught In The Crossfire
by Kate Edwards-Kearney

She floats along in smoky song,
the world singing to her beat.
A coy smile appears,
she'll tap and tap,
out come the lies.
Sooner you realise,
the world falls to her feet.

But she fell, my babe,
fell dark and haunted paths.
The sunshine in her step,
bitter victory laps.

I saw her in the Cale once,
her centre far as ever,
heart-broken stomping mermaid,
but I'll give her she is clever.
I'll sue you all, she sang,
and danced around the hosp,
and out she came,
to ruin my life again.

Would You Really See Me?
by Kitty Kane

If I came to meet you, what would you see?
Would you see what you wanted?
Or would you really see me?
Can I ever be, truly good for you,
Or will I eventually break you apart too?
My soul is broken, my body as well,
There may be truths of myself that I never will tell.
I hurt all those, that cross my path,
I don't wish it, I seem to have it down to an art.
When I look inside myself, it's hard to see,
What is light, and what is dark what truly is me.
My mind turns over, and over again,
Never still in its turmoil, always needing that friend.
I don't choose to be, the way I've become,
Life may be mapped, battles lost and battles won.
But if I could return, to the beginning once more,
I wouldn't be like this, on that I am sure.
Why do our lives play out the acts that they do?
I wish I knew that, and I'd share it with you.
We live with the scars, we acquire through life,
The marks of our living, our loving, our strife.
How long must we carry these marks both seen and not?
Will our minds ever, have truthfully forgot?
Life is a lesson, a lecture, an art,
But where our lives stay mostly, is deep in the heart.
So I may break you, hurt you and destroy you,
But I know that I'll try, to with my whole self-love you.
If you choose, to take that chance on me,
Maybe this time, I can let happiness be.

Crash Course Love
by Kristina V Griffiths

He is my southern comfort
Like the fire burning whiskey
His name catches in my throat.
And when I look in to his eyes
I want to scream and shout
That I cannot disguise
The way I feel
It's like my two hands gripping to lock the steering motion
On the wheel that attaches my heart to my thoughts.
I press my foot down on the break
Before my mouth opens
Without engaging my brain and words spill out
And causes chaos
And I slip in a pool of my mistakes
It is only then that the flashing red light
Flickers down
And the hazard blinkers dim
The impact
Of my body when it crashes in to sobriety with the realisation
That it is only made in the likeness of immortality
And the flash photography
Of the collision when my heart speaks its mind
Comes with police tape
And the warning sign
Do not drink and drive.

Recall of a Love
by Kristina V Griffiths

White horses venture with vigour-
across paths of sand dunes,
in a sleepy town,
where a glass pop bottle of youth
lies silent,
while upon candy clouds,
memories pass by.

I've tried to memorise,
names and faces
of those fragile human forms,
that are encased inside my Cortex lobe,
yours...
is the jigsaw piece,
that I cannot place.

I am haunted,
by the complications and distractions,
that traipse through the vortex,
masquerading as truthful knowledge.
My tongue misfires,
shooting off words,
that have no relevance,
but sting like salt in an open wound.

There are places I just can't reach,
and evermore the context of the words,
that pass from your lips,
outstretch the meaning,
of the cross-stitched conversation,
between Myself
and my former youth.

Faded lines between fiction and reality,
ware thin,
and grey matter overlaps,
I cannot recall...
the image of your face disintegrates from my mind,
and I sit in a bewildered blissful state,
with the illusion
that Tulips are more alive dead.

Little Fires
by LM Cooke

The central heating belches steam.
The house is warm,
But the place beside me on the sofa is cold,
And the stars upon which I wish
Were dead a billion years before I was born.

Such a little fire that burned
And burns no more.
Such heat it radiated,
Now extinguished.
And the world keeps on turning,
Though I am not sure how.

**The Watcher
by LM Cooke**

She shines like a beacon
And the air is charged
And the hair raises on the back of my neck.

She pulsates like a sickness
I breathe her toxic air
It saturates my blood with her celestial virus.

Who are you?
Why do you call?
Why do I respond?

When all I can do is clench my fists impotently,
Frown and laugh together.
And fear and flail and fail to act.

But all you can do is watch.
All you will do is watch.

Sonnet 2231
by Linda Angel

I do not claim to know the shapes of love;
Do cotton cumuli hearts manifest?
Perhaps it's that I'm cautious, wary of
My heartbeat sounding nothing like the rest.
Because no frames of reference may be found,
It could be that I don't know how love's done;
My wax it melts and settles on the ground;
As I am Icarus, I'm my own sun.
No feathers left; impossible to fly
Without direction, flight's forever lost
With intervention I shall skim the sky
As I become the 'Me' that love forgot.

I may not know the curvature of love;
But I shall board the flight till life takes off.

There
by Linda Angel

Give me two minutes alone with his lips and
I'll take him to places that hadn't existed
And that's where he'll see
what his heart means to me ...

For there he shall find
What his soul means to mine.

No Time for Goodbyes
by Leanne Cooper

Let the waves run crimson
Their ebb and flow in synch
with my fast fading pulse.
I have died alone too many times
to bat an eye at this latest disaster -
drowned in many a tidal wave before now.
Let me sink into the warmth
No time for goodbyes.

This is Not a Cry for Help
by Leanne Cooper

This is not a cry for help.
We have long passed the point of subtle hints
And dark thoughts veiled in jokes.
No, this is not a cry for help.
When begging for someone to listen has failed
And no one wanted to know;
Remember …
This is no longer a cry for help

Jade
by Leanne Cooper

Adorable gummy smiles beam the purest of sunshine from a cherubic face.
Mischievous and wild, you are my little howling wolf cub.
Your personality belies your appearance;
A little devil with angelic features:
Jewelled blue eyes, and golden, strawberry kissed hair.
When all my world collapsed around me,
You were the hope that kept me grounded.

Alone I pray.

The Butcher, Baker and Candlestick Maker
by Leanna Locker

Said the Butcher to the Baker - "I'll give you a wager,
I'll be dead by the end of the day.
I murdered my wife, my trouble and strife
Her body I can't hide away".
Said the Baker to the Butcher - "I think I can help you,
I need new meat to bake in my pies.
So, if her body's still fresh then cut off her flesh
And her body I'll help you disguise.
As for the fat, I can solve that
By asking the Candlestick Maker
Who's hard up on cash making candles that last,
To help out this friendly old Baker
By dipping his wicks to make candle sticks in human fat rather than pig.
The bones we can bury or sell to make money
And make a killing quite big!"

So, rubber-dub-dub three men in a tub, and who do you think they be?
A Butcher, a Baker, a Candlestick Maker - dealing in death all three.

Reality Check
by Lesly Finn

Where is she,
the 'me' I used to be?
Fading, shredding, wafting free
in ragged pieces, desperately
spinning, shrinking, hard to see.
Pretending, as things become less clear,
that nothing's wrong, I am still here.

Inside I sigh
and tell physicians passing by
'I'm not the same, although I try,
I'm crawling where I used to fly.'
The truth is hid in their reply,
'few treatment options for a brain'.
- I know I can't be 'me' again.

What Can't Be Cured
by Lesly Finn

Today the wine of life turned bitter.
Pain seeped into my mind and heart
with the almond flavor
of bespoke poison
and I cannot tell from
where it came.
I only know that its colour
is the deepest, darkest blue
and I must close my eyes
for fear that I may drown.

Bright hope, that giver of strength,
left yesterday by a different door.
While patience, at an end with indecision,
pride and self-delusion,
followed closely behind.
And, just as a dying flower cannot
help but lose its petals and decay,
so must I lay down my weary head
and face despair.

Valkyrie Dreamer
by Linda M. Crate

I will crash through
their dark ceilings
because I am a magic of light
sent to destroy nightmares
because I am the dreamer who is also
the keeper of golden moons
shining brighter than the sun,
and they made a mistake of waking
the dark beasts in me;
so now it is time to put to sleep
their monsters—
I am the Valkyrie
my white feathers will dance
through their black
until void is the only one that sings their name
for a time until even it forgets
because I refuse to remain here in this pain and rage
I was made for more than simply existing
will find my niche in life and will blind them all with my light
because I know those who speak ill of me
are already behind me,
but there's no need to look behind my shoulders
the past is in the past;
so, I will take the roots of this moment
bloom into a flower
they'll never cut down because I am too rooted in who I am to
lose myself.

Flood of Light
by Linda M. Crate

I do not fear the darkness
of night,
but of my own soul;
there is a darkness, there is an anger
burning as bright as my love and mercy
I do not want to lose myself
to this fury but I cannot eradicate it
it is always there
just want to cut it out of my heart—
night has stars and moonlight
so, I must believe
that even my soul has some redemption
even in its darkest moments,
but I don't always know;
sometimes
my mind takes dark turns and thinks awful things
I don't want to happen yet why did I think them to begin
with?
humans are all paradoxes,
but sometimes I don't even understand myself;
perhaps it's too much to ask for love
because how can we offer a perfect understanding
of others when we fail to grasp ourselves
for who we are?
and, yet, even in the darkest moments
my hopes and my dreams keep flooding over me and my love
a flood of light
comes to burn away all the darkness.

Turning Nightmares to Dust
by Linda M. Crate

Light dancing in the universe
I prefer night
because the moon is my mother,
and she seems softer
than the sun
whose light can scald and burn;
her song is kinder
I think than the compassion of the sun
which seems fickle—
and she understands me better
she knows that I have darkness and light
in me,
and they both make up
the yin and yang of who I am;
a delicate balance
I prefer to be life, truth, and love
sometimes, however,
one must be a destroyer so I destroy nightmares
I will never be a dying star fading into the sky
because I am immortal of the flame
refusing to descend into the heart of darkness
I won't be a monster even in my darkest moments
will simply strike out the eyes of every
vile thing that exists to smash in
upon my dreams—
I will only use every unkindness
as a stepping stone,
will only bite when I have to;
because I prefer giving my flowers and my moons but if
they provoke me I will have no problem
scorching them in my sun until all of their nightmares are dust.

In My Dreams
by Lynn White

I have such beautiful dreams
inside my head.

Inside my head.
Struggling to get outside
into the ragged, jagged
outside life
which passes for normality.

Such beautiful dreams.

Such a perfect life
lying inside my head.
I would like it to be
on the outside.

Sunrise
by Lynn White

The rock looms large above me,
the petrified remains of the last time the sun burned
in the time of giants.
Giant rocks and giant creatures fused together in the fire.
Look!
I'm climbing now
Higher and higher.
Now I'm lit by moonlight,
but soon the sun will rise
and consume us,
fuse us together
the rock and I.
I am not sure anything will remain
after.

**Sometimes There's Magic
by Lynn White**

See that raindrop
falling,
falling,
falling into wetness.
You see it falling,
a silvery teardrop
then it disappears
into wetness,
becomes invisible.
Is that magic?
Only
if it could choose invisibility,
or choose to stay
a raindrop.

That would be magic.

Lost
by Marianne Burgess

I still don't know where I am going
But I'm going;
I don't know where I belong
Till I am there;
I don't know how to rid my heart
Of all the sorrow;
Or climb above this mountain
Of despair;
I don't know how the future feels
But I will feel it;
I must endure the pain that I am
Feeling now;
But it won't last - I'll mend my
Broken pieces;
I'll glue myself together again
Somehow;
And tomorrow will be brighter
Than today is;
Peace and quiet will surely
Help the mind;
I'll search for joy to fill my
Soul again;
And those sad memories will
All be left behind...

So Lonely
by Marion Feasey

So lonely, so lonely, if only, if only
someone would talk to me.
If I heard the right words
and the meanings weren't blurred,
it would end this deep misery.
Character deflation, total isolation.
I feel like a lesser being.
Rejected, neglected, socially disconnected.
This is the person I'm seeing.

So lonely, so lonely, if only, if only
I could break out of this shell.
I'm empty of feeling
and life has no meaning.
I need to rise out of this hell.
I'm alone, so alone, can't cope on my own.
Please somebody hear what I say.
I need some advice to make me think twice
before throwing my life away.

Life and Death
by Marion Feasey

Your life was just a parody of all things rich and grand
and why you lived above your means I fail to understand.
Death always lingered near you - he pursued you for so long.
You refused to hear his calling, but you knew his mournful song.
You chose to ignore the tell-tale signs when your life was excess and greed,
and even when death stood beside you - no warnings were you going to heed.
Death greeted you in this meadow - your final resting place.
You took your last breath and looked up at death as he held you in final embrace.
In life you lay in this same meadow, gazing up at English blue skies,
but now you see only blackness, as the crow peck out your eyes.
Now the roar of the traffic continues, from the main road that passes close by.
For nobody witnessed your passing and nobody heard your last cry.
Now bees and flies buzz round your corpse and ground beetles sing and dance.
As the earth devours your very soul - life won't get a second chance.
You filled your life with sheer pretence and wove a web of lies.
So in the end you had not one friend to care about your demise.
So nobody's going to miss you - they won't even remember your face,
and we will all breathe a sigh of relief and the world will be a better place.

Mr Hide
by Matthew Cash

Constantly running from that fella within,
The dastardly deviant tempter of sin.
He whispers quietly from the space behind my head,
Promising this is last time that he'll need to be fed.
One muttered sentence is all that it takes,
For so few words so many mistakes.
A deluge of gluttony, a widening crack,
Endless debauchery, all sealed by his pact.
Mr Hide beckons, persuades and he wins,
The dastardly deviant tempter of sins.
And here in the aftermath awash with regret,
Self-hatred, repulsion, guilt and the want to forget.
But no sign of the deviant now he's had his way,
Rapacious and wanton my will he doth slay.
He will hide and leave me alone on the ground,
Used and abused beneath my own burial mound.
But he will be back and yes he might win,
This dastardly deviant tempter of sin.

Last Night I Said "I Love You"
by Matthew Cash

Last night I said "I love you," as usual,
I expected her answer, as usual,
It came slightly delayed, unusual,
The flu had debilitated her despite my refusal.

Yesterday she said she wished she were dead,
This was nothing new, a catchphrase re-said,
As she lay on the sofa-made bed.

This morning she laid in, a usual thing,
Saved for weekends or Bank Holiday morning.
I took her a mug and expected a hug,
But she was comatose, not even a shrug.
I placed the tea down on the cupboard beside,
Not realising then that my mother had died.

Although this was worse, just partial physical death,
Who knows what was inside still taking a breath,
Stroke is too nice a word for this evil conjunction,
Death's black velvet glove coaxing malfunction.

Paralysed from the neck down,
Shut up inside, inwardly drown,
I prayed for her death from day one to day seven,
And then thank you God she took the expressway to Heaven.

Sinister Grins
by Matt Humphries

We play these games
On streets we don't recognise
Avoiding sinister gents with twisted grins
The Status Quo burns in their eyes
Cash signs where the pupils lie
Another brick in walls of lucre
Riches lie in altruistic prisons

We're lost and bound but never see
A need to take our place in history
To be the generation who breaks free
With a fleeting glimpse of honesty

Are we really as bad as them?
Do we not grab all we can?
Do we not want to end the war on want?
Do we complain or hit the streets
Or accept our lot, admit we lost

While we sink
Their wealth multiplies
Stored offshore from prying eyes
Are we all Daniel Blake?
Destined to work until we drop dead
The fleeting glimpse of honesty
Is the difference between our claims?
The colour of money and sinister grins.

What we Like?
by Matt Humphries

We like to believe
We like to point
We like to put their noses
Out of joint
We like to frame
We instigate
The change we want to see
We like to march
We like protests
Our lives are better for what went
We like to scream
We like to shout
Until our lives improve for the best
We like to dream
We like to hope
We like to write the future script
As we grow old
As we retire
Will the world even be here?

**The Sands of Time Divide
by Matt Humphries**

The brainwashed masses
Never really understand
Their brains are fried
By daytime telly
Drip fed nonsense
From daily newspapers
Persuaded to vote
For their captors
They work in jobs
That they despise
To create the wealth
For corporate pride
Swallowing the lies
Refusing to wake
The motto they swallow
Is I'm alright Jack
Their kept in position
By the privileged few
Keeping them down
Not knowing what to do
All the time it's slipping by
The sands of time divide.

Emily, Come and Take Your Place in the Human Race.
by Matt Nunn

Don't choke the silent volumes of strangeness
that buys the hurt currencies allowing us to be free.

Fling off the void veils of mute shuffling sleeps
seething with discomforting thesis' on dreams.

Release the bitter songbird morbidly entrapped
within the discarded lost romantic choruses
you store your shrunken self-inside, waiting to mourn

for what never comes.

Realising it's just the beginning, finish the end
and live fully in its deletion.

Be enigmatically prideful to own your enigma.

Everyday Disappointment
by Matt Nunn

Since I was diagnosed as the raging source of all disappointments
spitting black dots of death upon the blue skies in familial portraits of togetherness,
for the shame I bring, mum stone- cast –in- gargoyle- face
can't bring herself to look at, or hate me
and dad needs to absolve himself abusively by clouting me about
for not trying on the proudly inherited Neanderthal act,

rather than reaching for that overdone line by Larkin,
now reduced to meaning no more than a t-shirt slogan,
I load up on Cobain and splash my brains,
as if they were merely ingredients in a casually flung trifle,
all over the martyrs eternally queuing outside the after-life.

But every day to prove exactly who and what I am, I miss,
leave myself limbo stranded,
like an uncertain question asked to a world full of definite answers.

Bird Feeder
by Maureen Weldon

Her hand had just been kissed,
each kiss like the roses cascading
over the partition wall

or the hideous fence that must be broken.
Neighbours: the sort who hate
without reason.

Her hand had just been kissed.
Does it matter that the horrid man
frightened away her long awaited birds?

Their small bungalow now loaded with books –
very precious.
Yet the hideous fence still stands.

'Do one. Do one,' he yells

Resistance
by Michael Carter

All night the spotlight moon
interrogated me: guilty or not?
What will the spring melt reveal and
what's in the freezer? They want
fingerprints, evidence of the handled.
There are different kinds of prisons
and all of them count for something.
Prison of bestowal.
The prison of Hikmet, Madelstam,
the witness outside, *I can.* The prison
of the body with its lumps and gasses, hunger
guarding everything. Waking up to a clutch
of daffodils, the dog still asleep.
The prison of satisfy, of lunacy.
The prison like a pen
you can't get the top off.

Salt
by Michael Carter

Of salt and longing
the whole city's Lot's wife –
to return or remember?

What casts darkness in all
this bright? Cutouts, black forms.
Low winter sun and everyone's

shadowed to silhouette. The sidewalk
is glare, is salt and ice.

Snowfall
by Michael Carter

The stop sign grew a halo of snow
Like the headpiece of a medieval Madonna in a world turned
White, almost every surface sculpted in a rapture
Of white. Isn't it time we find
Another word for people
and what we call the dark? How can we call
people dark and darkness the dark of days
in the same light? Snow blind in
a spring storm. The light
is blinding, is white.

Beneath the Shallows
by Michael Cronogue

Gravel churning
As silt envelopes like a cloak,
The Ammonite sits patiently
Keen senses, sharpened to warn
Of friend or foe alike.
Turning inward,
Its ribbed edges spiralled
In a downward arc, foetal-like for protection
Or, is it a prelude to attack?
Predator or prey, hunter or hunted
Each movement is like
A performing melodrama.
The current creates an ambience
As it ripples along the tidal flow,
Time marches on:
Relentless, unstoppable,
Oblivious to the theatre
Being played out therein.
Where does this story end?
As the silt clears, battle lines become drawn
Each must to their own endeavour;

And yet, all are destined to a Jurassic future.

Love Conquers Hate
by Michael Cronogue

Martin Luther King once famously did declare
He would rather stick with love, as
Hate was too great a burden to bear.
Yet in this world today we see nightly on TV
How this burden manifests itself, almost each and
everywhere.
Hatred spawns its rhetoric within the fibre of a nation
From east to west across the globe,
We seem locked in perpetual confrontation.
Voices of reason get marginalised to the side
And wiser heads cannot prevail, on this sickening situation.
When folk become targets due to the colour of their skin
Where accent and origin results in vile abuse,
These actions only feed the evil of human sin.
When we allow ourselves to forget the rule of universal love,
Like vultures anarchy circles, waiting for it to begin.
And when we look for leadership we only find despair,
As those tasked with seeking peace
Seem more concerned with the styling of their hair,
Preferring the language of Armageddon,
Rather than debate we might all share.
But the voices of resistance have once again been stirred,
Those protesting to power have made this declaration:
Love conquers hate, on this we've always concurred
But to love your neighbour as yourself is once again,
The message that needs to be heard.

Unselfish Love
by Nerisha Kemraj

You didn't have to force yourself
You didn't have to lie
I heard it in your voice
I saw it in your eyes

What was written on your face,
was what you felt inside
What your lips didn't say
was, you were no longer mine

So, I'm giving you your space
Take all the time you want
Just don't take too long,
lest you should wake
to find that I am gone

Then too, it may be for the better
I won't hinder your growth
I won't tug at your heart-strings
To me, there's nothing you owe

You tried your best for us
You gave me all your love
I couldn't be the one for you
It's sad how this ended up

I wish the best for you
With everything I have
And who knows,
maybe we'll fall back in love...

Immobile
by Nerisha Kemraj

Turning back the hands of time,
would things work out some other way
had I chosen different?
Trying to step in a new direction
to make things work but
thoughts bring forth hindrance.

Should I stay or should I go,
lest I should lose it all?
I'm caught between the two.
On either side mountains loom,
a raging river in between

Music in the distance
An air of melancholy,
adding to my blues
The horn blows,
and a clock rings in a new hour

The road forks out,
waiting to be tread on
Stuck where I am,
my decision holds me back
My fear of the unknown.

**Night Sadness
by Norbert Gora**

The dusk came
between the clouds
emphasizing the name
of icy darkness
sad moments I'm witnessing
when can be seen
a spectacle of falling tears
of a lonely night.

The soul as calm
as the foamed ocean
during the day
now yells
sobs tighten the tongs
on the weakened throat.

I'm trying
to turn this pain
into syllables
in vain, this is
logorrhea of the cruel fate.

World Full of Anxiety
by Norbert Gora

Dark clouds of changes
took over the sky
in the gloomy fluffs
are hidden drops of human dread.

Fiery bird of death
roared over the blue of the Loire
the faces of tri-color
saw the devil of new, dangerous times.

Munich demon
spread the wings of destruction
decorated the concrete trail
with the soulless bodies

Forced to live
in the world full of anxiety
we, divine caricatures
quietly sneak
along the pages of the book
of appalling future.

on the corner of tomorrow
can be seen another verse
is it an angel of happiness?
or a fiend of our undoing
nobody knows.

The Unforgiven
by Paul Beech

Well past middle-age,
bald,
he sits there with his love,
milkshakes –
his banana, hers vanilla –
as midnight drizzle beyond the pane
slicks the black tarmac
of the car park
of this garishly neon-lit
deserted
retail park,
a daughter's email on his mind.

Cast out
for seeking happiness with his late love,
he sips through a straw,
smiles,
a kiss on the back of his hand,
some old rock number playing,
a kiss on his lips this time,
her brown eyes forever his world now,
his joyous world now,
the Unforgiven.

I Hope
by Paul B Morris

I hope, that you are happy now,
I hope, you are now well,
I hope, you've now found a way to be,
I hope, you are free from your hell.

I hope, I live a life so long,
I hope, that my battles are now won,
I hope, demons allow me some respite,
I hope, I can be something to my Son.

I hope, my mind becomes less clouded,
I hope, feelings start to give,
I hope, dreams don't sterilise existence,
I hope, the world finally begins to live.

I hope, you will not turn away,
I hope, that you one day open your eyes,
I hope, life doesn't have to be like this,
I hope, you're not blinded by the lies.

Disconnected
by Paul B Morris

Hey there, are you now free?
could you listen, to me for a while?
as all is not going too well,
I really do not feel, like being me.

My word is turning so cold and black,
leaving me scared at my own reflection,
I'm not being overly dramatic,
but, you should really know, I'm about to crack.

Really worried that I can now only see the end,
suicidal imagery, driving towards a complete overload,
forcing me to greatly reconsider everything,
whilst hoping that I am something you can mend.

I'm disconnected - from everything that you see,
mind pollution - is slowly seeping into me,
disconnected – from the life that I need,
cannot rest – until my broken mind is freed.

All is not well with me, are you here?
can you not hear me screaming?
lost inside my own colourful, personal hell,
medication doesn't work, serving only to increase my fear.

Daily nightmares, force me to scrape at my skin,
I'm clearly falling to my knees now my precious,
please help me to make amends,
can you save me from the thoughts within?

How can everyone be so ignorant and blind?
irrelevantly stating how well I look,
but, that is the fault in its entirety,
for my illness exists totally 'in my mind'.

I'm disconnected - from everything you see,
mind destruction - slowly taking over me,
disconnected - as life slowly passes me by,
don't be too sad – everyone has their time to die.

Down
by Paul B Morris

My thinking is blinkered, my head begins to hurt,
So useless and worthless, I'm buried in the dirt.

I'm prostrate before you, falling to my knees,
Submissive dismissive, help me wont you please?

So sorry I worry, that this will drag you down,
Feel guilty please be free, why don't you let me drown.

You're talking keep going, it really is so kind,
Something yet nothing, so I can free my mind.

These tired views of past life, they slowly turn to hate,
I should ignore them dissolve them, so they don't seal my fate.

I'm hating this mirror, because it distorts my eyes,
Keeps showing me nothing, other than a life of lies.

The darkness this greyness, it occupies my mind,
Without you to love me, I'm feeling lost and blind.

Thoughtful Dread
by Paul J Elias

A plague. Curse. A mind obsessed.
A mind feverishly possessed, which insanity has lovingly caressed.
Fear. Terror. Every thought common sense refusing
Access to my twirling, swirling musing, thoughts deep, dark, impressions brooding, confusing.
Anxiety. Horror. Thoughts vivid, then confused, obscure.
Reasoning my inner demons abjure, but with regret, find affection, succour.
Life. Existence, if such it be of battles internal,
Of tortures eternal, of dreams of death, of realms infernal.
Torments that eternal screams,
Nightmares, feverish dreams, that God refuses to redeem.
Thoughts. Yearnings. Longings for blood.
Darkest deeds, a demonic flood, a mind in torment misunderstood.
Deep requirements, shaded needs,
Thoughts of death grow, breeds, a fulfilment of darkest deeds.
Stagnant murmurs, engendered of hate, violently repressed.
Constant war to keep suppressed, lest loosed an anger a horror possessed.
Descends upon a world of prey.
Washed in a blood-soaked bouquet, of death, pain, of decay.
If allowed to roam free from my mental abyss,
Then my thoughts would be free to caress, to kiss, in an orgy of horrific bliss.
So, control I keep of a mind misunderstood,
To protect like a normal mind would, to save a world from thoughts of blood.

Hidden Shame
by Paul John Elias

I hide the shame behind veils of smiles.
Buried deep, beneath ID and psyche.
I dare not speak of that which reviled,
My fragile ego, with which I strike,
A pose of unadulterated glee.
The darkness is solely mine to see.

I run at night, through my weary dreams.
Through gossamer threads of my own troubled sanitary.
A tormented soul, which silently screams,
At images conjured from my thought filled depravity.
My cries, plaintive, forever lost in silence loud,
Screaming beneath my torturous, mental shroud.

'Is this me' externally echoes my own vanity.
What is it I have lost to be so utterly broken.
My mind crushes my believed insanity,
Better ignored, hidden, than freely spoken.
Yet fears are hiding beneath the smiles,
Of stubborn vanity, that psyche reviles.

It is pain, with which my ego easily copes.
It is but to ourselves to whom we lie.
Burying deep, beneath dark, forlorn hopes,
Where not the wings of truth may fly.
Hidden deep, beneath a mantle of forced normality.
Beyond the bounds of our own rationality.

Forces, which assault the decaying, mental walls,
Erected in defence of deep, obsidian despair,
Breaks through to infest gloom laden halls,
Of an inner mind, now open, stripped bare
Searching for the smallest, briefest hope filled light,
Quenching hope beneath a tidal wave of night.

Epic battles of assorted chemical infusions.
Discourse amongst the knowing few.
Beaten, battered, left with nothing but confusion.
So deep and dark, if they truly knew.
Would they unbidden rise, nod and silently leave.
To abandon me to the loss of the hope I grieve.

I Need You to See Me
by Paul Raynsford

Why is it you do not see
Past the smile
Past the dry eyes
at what lies beyond
the broken man
Scared and alone
in a world of darkness

You claim you care
you claim you love me
yet you fail to see
Past the smile
Past the dry eyes
at what lies beyond

Inside I am screaming for help
yet all you see is the mask I wear

The smile the dry eye
these are but a mask
for inside I am broken
and screaming out for help

For I am lost
in a world of darkness
I am standing on the edge
Ready to fall over

Here I am screaming out
I need you
I need you to save me
I need you to help me
Find me again

I may appear strong and proud
But truly I am lost and broken

I need you to Look beyond the smile
I need you to Look beyond the dry eyes
I need you to see the tears
I need you to see the fear
I need you to see the pain
I need you to see me for me

But yet all you see
is the radiant smile and the dry eyes
of the mask I wear

Why can you not see
I need you
Look beyond the mask I wear
And you will see
you are my all
you are my saviour

Without you I cannot go on
without you I will fall
without you I will fail

So please I need
You to see
beyond the mask
and see me for me.

There was a Time
by Paul Raynsford

There was once a time
When I could look
Upon the mirror
And there I would see
Myself smiling back.
Now here I stand
Staring upon the mirror
Yet the person
Looking back at me
No longer smiles.
Looking back is a person
That I no longer recognize
There staring back at me
Is nothing but a stranger
Who looks lost and scared
He looks alone in
a word of pain and hurt
I can see the darkness that surrounds
There is a man lost
Not only to himself
But to all around him as well
Confused and alone
He no longer recognizes anyone
Not his friends not his family
Not even his own children
Are recognizable to him anymore
He is lost in a world
created by his mind
Created by his illness.

My Fight With Depression
by Paul Raynsford

Here I am down again
lower than low
mentally drained
emotionally broken
walking among the shadows
as though life has no meaning.

Here I am again
asking myself
where did I wrong
why do I feel so alone
why do I push everyone away.

But all I really need is there support
this is my fight with depression.

A battle with my mind
that little voice in my head
telling me over and over
that they will all be ok,
they will all be better off
once I am gone.

That little voice in my head
telling me today is the day
the day to end it all

Each day I fight with my depression
and each day I survive
but will the fight ever end
can I ever truly win?

Or is that voice in my head
really me being realistic
telling it to myself as it is

should today really be the day
will they all really be ok
will they all really be better off
should I end it all today
this is a question that I ask myself
a million times a day.

Embers
by Pippa Bailey

The ember of ideas is born from the darkest depths.

Fragile thoughts, a string of words that cascades from an eloquent tongue.
Idle notions which bore deep into the sanctity of our hearts, ignite that spark.
That ember.

You were there at the beginning, and you'll stay with me to the end.
A collection of persuasive declarations your tapestry, weft, adrift in a sea of ideas.
Your ember.

A fire so deep it ignites the blackness of my soul, a blistering, smoulder of pleasure and sin.
I give myself to the burn, warmth of twisted bodies. A subconscious meld of stitched emotion.
Our ember.

A gnawing hunger for you.
You're a feast for the mind, my biting need that gouges scars in warped clarity.
Senses smothered, I quake on my knees.
A simple idea prolongs the carnality of release.
Indulging in the bitter sweet suffering of tortured silence.
Teeth marks on tender flesh, a steady rope that twists and burns.
Arched silhouettes dance into the night.
You, the darkness to my light.
My ember.

Flying with the Music
by Rachel Arnold

Shattered into pieces, falling down the abyss, no bottom, no end,
Broken in many ways, will I ever mend?
Music, lovingly held my hand, and said, "I will always be your friend…"
"I know the language that holds people together
So, get up, stay with me, and you will smile forever…."

But,
I am not just the sounds that bring you lots of pleasure,
So, you can play your records, whatever the weather,
Dancing chords of delight, minds reaching an octave higher
Our voice souring with the notes, happiness we remember,

So
You think you've been broken, you think you've been hurt
You think you are stamped right down in the dirt
Well, each little piece of you, that you thought was going to rust,
Was actually a little note at rest, gathering a little bit of dust
A broken heart that is in little pieces
Are words of a new song for new concerts and releases
Music came and told me this first thing in the morning
As when I woke, I had a brand-new feeling, dawning
My pieces had been rearranged
Like a new symphony, had been explained,
An orchestra of angels lifted me high, with sonorous wings
As a great powerful firebird, but who gently sings
We flew over the roof tops and colourful valley's all night,
Music travels, passes through walls, when there is no sight
Some people shout, "Will you turn that down, I can't get to sleep"
But I carried on flying over cities, and grave yards, without getting the creeps

Hordes of people were lying in their beds
Torn from many countries, their hearts having bled
But they still sing, they still dance
They are safe with me the music, they have a chance

I am not just the sounds that sing out from the telly
I get boxed, packaged and sold into something smelly
But actually

I am freedom
I can't be tamed
I am everywhere
I am not ashamed
I move around in the air
I can touch you, when you're not there
I make you feel alive, yes you do still care
I am music
I am free
Welcome back to humanity..

Treasures of the Mind
by Rachel Arnold

The mind is a treasure trove
Waiting to open, in a box of the infinite sea
At the bottom of the ocean, lies the real me

Ideas sparkle as sapphire's, on an elegant neck
Kind thoughts shine like rubies, laid across a dull dress
Dreams are like rainbows after a storm
Whether in colour, or black and white
The mundane routine they adorn

The mind is full of memories that one holds dear
The love of a lost one, is still alive, behind a tear
A million thoughts pass through a day of a year
While clothes wear away, and outside there is fear

The mind can travel, when your hidden out of sight
Answers to questions, spring like flowers, when its quiet
Deep in the mind treasures lie
It's when you sit still and don't ask why

The world has its status, addictions
Money out-money in
But the gifts of my character
Bud from deep within
My gifts are in the world when people see them to have
How they view them, or capture them
In hate or in love
I wouldn't have them if I didn't water them with good teachings and time
As struggle and battles surround me
I know with certainty
The treasures of the mind

At Peace
by Rachel Melia

Fields full of yellow flowers in bloom
Little birds dart around us
No worries or cares to bring gloom
Peace and tranquillity instils in me
This journey is calm and relaxing
I drink in the views
This time is precious
And I cherish it dearly.

Overwrought
by Rachel Melia

Why do I care?
What you think of me
Do you even realise
How it makes me feel?
Big knot in my tummy
Sleepless nights
Overthinking
Brain in overdrive
Irrational thoughts
Out of control
Overreacting
To every detail
Words cut deeper
Than any sharp tool
Think before you speak
My advice to you
Myself, I'll put pen to paper
Write a few words.

Little Me
by Rachel Melia

I'm 4ft nothing
But don't underestimate me
I'm tougher than I look
On the surface in any case
I'm like the cowardly lion
I carry a purse full of courage
Armed with a pencil as my sword
The paper is my shield
I have a big heart
That often gets bruised
But I paint on my red lipped smile
To face the world once more.

Parts of Me
by Red Gibson

At peace with the chaos consuming my dreams that absorb the kindness into chaos and toxicity until it's nothing but a living nightmare. I am at peace because I don't have a choice.
I have burned myself out with every ounce of strength, I know that this is now just part of me.

The depths of the dark claw out and pull me under, drowning my cries of isolation with shouts of anger. I hear the frustration of every demon that consumes me and I am at peace.
I am exhausted, so drained. I don't know how else to be. This is just a part of me.
This isn't betrayal of the light in my soul because I am being positive by accepting the situation for what it is. I am diseased by an atrocity of morose memories of all the ways in which I have been hurt.

Don't be fooled. It hurts. But I'm still breathing.
I am alive. And I can feel. So much emotion until the point of numbness.
I scatter apart into fragments of sad AND good.
The gloom consumes more than the other, but it's not really all that there is. And I am at peace because all of the cruelty of a haunted mind is just a part of me. I accept this. I accept me.

I am still breathing. I am still here. It can be so isolating but, it's all just parts of me.

Impaled
by Red Gibson

A knife
with its' gleaming point
searing into my flesh
with the hands of my own control
is better than the blade
that is hoisted into my back
by the hands of another.

To impale me between my wings
removes my ability to fly
but I accept this fatality
for I see no light left
only remainders of grey
I have been decaying slowly
since the moment he touched me.

I am merely a walking corpse now.

People are temporary
but the scars leave a residue
that turn the most kindest of hearts
into cold souls.
I inspire in the way I encourage
the creative to write verse.

But the touch I have on myself
is the touch everyone has shown me-
I am not worth anything.

I am hurting too much
so I will shred myself until I feel raw
& eventually feel nothing at all.

I am floating. Drowning. Fading.
Simply a ghost.

I Can Feel (Assault Survival)
by Red Gibson

I can feel his hands on me, gripping
blood gushing between my thighs,
remnants of bruises on my cheeks
and I try to pull away
but then I'm placed in a chokehold
and then I can't breathe.
I am terrified.
My friends tell me that he's charming
That I'm lucky, that I
Should bring him along.
But I don't like him, I don't want him.
I am so alone.
And I will disguise the wounds he placed,
as self-harm, because I feel to blame.
Thus, I'll start cutting again.
It goes from fear to anger to emptiness

Pay the Ghosts
by Richard Archer

All my life I've been haunted by the ghosts I should have paid,
Pursuing me to get payment for all the mistakes I made.
I really don't want to start to add up the cost
So I can only try to guess at how much will be lost.
The ghosts come at night so I can't sleep I pace the floor,
Angrily they pound at my windows and doors.
Gaping mouths screaming that I should let them in
So they can finally collect the payment for my many sins.
Every night they wear me down, I fumble for the window catch
Wondering if this night, I finally settle my debts and make it my last.
But I know that as always by the time the night is through
I still won't have found the courage to pay my ghosts their dues.
Even knowing all the tortures that I could save,
This coward is certain he will take his debts to his grave.

Wish Fulfilment
by Richard Archer

The stars that we all wish upon each night are all dead,
their last failing light has struggled to reach us.
While oblivious to their death throes, we cast our
tired cliched desires into the heavens towards them where

our wishes cluster like grumbling grey smog trails,
ominously pooling over towns and cities.
Verbal pollution launched by the lost
drifting towards dead pinpricks in the sky while

below we move on, uncaring, as once
a wish has been wished it's no longer our concern.
With no star to guide them our ailing aspirations slowly dissipate
bearing all that we ever hoped for away delicately

destroying the last desperate hopes of star-crossed lovers
softly killing the sweet secret dreams of sensitive shy boys and
smothering the pitiful cries of those crushed by their lives.
All hopelessly wished on the light from a dead star.

I'm Smiling on the Inside?
by Richard Archer

What if you just didn't feel like you can smile?
What if for you happiness feels like a trial?
What if you feel for your own real reasons,
You can't be one of life's shiny happy people.
Would you think to fit in that you had to fake it,
Put on a false smile that makes your face ache.
Hoping to fool people you're the life and soul,
But worried that if the truth is told.
That if you confess to friends your real mental state,
That if you reveal you don't think life is great.
As you tell them each day what you go through
Your so-called friends will harshly judge you.
Because of this each day you try to hide,
All the emotions slowly killing you inside.
So each morning you put on your familiar suit of lies,
Hoping that today no one will see through your disguise.

**Loving an Illusion
by Richard Beevor**

Walk soft the green grass,
warm in summer sun,
two people in a land
of lovers on the run.

My arm about your shoulders,
to protect against the world,
intense emotion of loves
cauldron in which we are hurled.

The needs of modern living
provide no way of escape,
break the bonds of reality
held together without shape.

I follow you down
to a tree in the meadow,
we sit in shade
from the suns glow.

Yet if I kiss your lips
in a moment so sincere,
I know the scene will change
and you will disappear.

Word Flowers
by Richard Beevor

Shallow words away
poet words speak then betray
buds of truth appear.

The Friend in my Head
by Richard Beevor

I have a friend
lives in my head,
he wishes me well
but he wants me dead!

My OCDs are calling
their passion is enthralling,
routine keeps me wired
hide's dementia it's not required.

In a voice so loud
my friend keeps speaking,
'What's that secret?
The one you are keeping!'

The need for less is straining,
these words I'm juggling and arranging,
memories so memorable,
times of such wonder,
distant though they be,
cast by life asunder.

My friend probes avenues in my past,
drives me crazy!
See's doors unopened
all memories now hazy.

The pounding rising higher,
hammer of the Gods lacks desire,
pictures coming into view,
who's that girl that I once knew?
The dark-haired beauty in a flyaway skirt,
changed my perspective ripped up my shirt,
touched me with strong feminine wiles,
reached out from within, discovered my trials.

Wild adventures all gone
my friend says I'm dying,
those pretty perfumed delights
nevermore trying.

Changing away crossing many streams,
discarded my promise and lost my dreams,
closing down the sentient noise sent away,
but still to remember and yearn for that day.

'You gave up all you were!'
says my friend in my head,
my day in the sun, now fragile shadows,
now dead.

The moments pass in a heartbeat of rage and fire,
my deep dark secret burns beneath awareness of desire,
the sun will no more shine on my passion now dead,
and all for the mistakes made by my friend in my head.

He berates me now with cries of
'You cannot pursue her life evermore!'
my secret lain deep, lain dark so low,
buried beneath this grim horror story of amour.

I have a friend lives in my head,
he has religious leanings,
destroyed my truth, took life away,
my love torn apart and given different meanings.

The friend in my head took her love away,
dissolved her face and hair gave me just a frame,
turned my life into a hollow shell,
left her broken, burnt her clothes, erased her name.

The friend in my head
knows that now I am dead.

Agency for Lost Souls
by Richard Proffitt

Tuesday morning at lovers leap
We discuss our terminal relationship
Fixating on your jewellery, I stumble over the words, trying to say,
trying to say,
I still need you
Without seeming 'needy'

Bitter sweet and sour all. Bird song – traffic
As always you are the strong one
Like a conquering Emperor, surveying his newly-won territory
You gesture me to the picnic bench
I'm on the back foot
You're simply, unruffled

This is the last time, you explain
And I see you have already made a splendid world, without me.
Now the Universe has played a trick on me and I
Don't know where I exist
I'm Out Of Time, leaching on to people and living on their taste,
proclivities, gestures, culture,
emotional states, and their personalities
It is extremely draining

A non-person-I
My other half lost somewhere
Five years will fly past and what is left of me will go through the
motions
I'll learn to live without vicarious desire
I shall find myself once more
I will re-learn my opinions
That's how it went before.

Dear Counsellor
by Richard Proffitt

'You need a little TLC', he said
Hmmm, I'd prefer THC, I thought…
He put his hand gingerly upon my knee, and smiled with his thin lips;
Try as I might I couldn't produce any tears for his benefit,
instead I sort of grimaced – an expression conveying emotional pain, I hoped.

The interview room was a cosy carpeted box,
The rain outside tapped pleasantly upon the window; autumn light penetrated weakly,
A box of tissues upon the table,
Should I even be here?
I'm not the world's first runaway

'So your parents threw you out of home?'
Sort of – now they want me back – but no – I won't go back, it doesn't feel like home anymore
Friends are letting me sleep on their sofa,
Temporarily
No money you see
No savings
I'd like a little bedsit of my own,
I don't know what I'm doing with my life
I'm just 17
Don't know what to do next
Cut off from my emotions
Feel numb

Should I tell you about the cannabis?
About the alcohol and the tranquilisers?
Should I tell you about the shoplifting and the criminal damage?
Should I tell you that I'm afraid of my own mind?

Crisis loan,
Fair rent officer
Income support,
Housing Benefit,
Estranged

Thank you for your Tender Loving Care
For your listening ear
For your support

Society does exist, despite what Thatcher says
Altruism does exist, despite our culture of selfish greed

And there'll come a time when I shall help others
As you have helped me.

Home Sanity Kit
by Richard Proffitt

I Wuz in the Whiskey Time Zone, thought I'd build a home sanity kit
One of these hidden bottles must be full…
Struck by the charm of yr missing tooth grin
And your 2inches of chest hair peeping over yr filthy t-shirt
No! Tell me! I can't guess your blood's secret
Or your first experience of love's tender embrace

Sleep in my bed tonight
It's better than yr broken down trailer
We'll beg up sum money for the apple tree's flat cider
Now 15 years are past
And you'll always be young

Inside my kit are pages from the bible,
Pages from the I Ching and yarrow sticks
A bottle of cheap whiskey and blues a-plenty
Tarot card portions and the Enochian keys
A trail of burnt tin-foil – razor blades and crow's feathers

I miss you, my prince of the street

The Weight of Space
by Roz Weaver

'Maybe you should take a nap'
I say
hoping it will confine your sadness
to just one room of the house
or how with your sleep
we find temporary peace.

You wonder how
I can spend so long
lying in the bath.
It's the only door with a lock on.
Sometimes it's my only escape.

If rooms had porous walls,
like a sponge
I'd beg them to soak up all your melancholy,
then saturated,
let it trickle out to the ground
and water seeds
who will blossom in its memory.

If it were mine,
I would give the sun to watch you glow,
because I'd rather live in darkness
my whole life
if it would just keep you warm.

Solitude
by Roz Weaver

Quiet, dear mind,
when thinking breaks you apart
cascade your confessions onto this page
till you come away empty.

Feel, dear heart,
numbing the strain does not soften the break
fear not the flood of sensations
for with your rhythmic beat they will dissipate.

Presence, dear body,
one day you will feel at one with yourself
and your reach will be infinite;
here you can tend to your trauma.

Freedom, dear soul,
rest with expectation for the next adventure
and leave behind everything
that resists your balletic wandering.

One for Sorrow
by Roz Weaver

Our minds have us believe terrible things
calmly convincing us we are not enough
like there is a shortage of oxygen
and not all are worthy of air.

You think I don't see
how your eyes drain of light
how you speak in riddles
and commit to me keepsakes
in case one of these days
you do it like you say you will
with a telephone goodbye
and shared tears
repeating 'I love you' in fierce faith
of its ability to resuscitate.

I will never forget,
up to my ankles in perfect white snow
the bloodcurdling mist of that graveyard
embracing your life
as I waited for those flashing blue lights
watching one lone magpie
fly above the graves
and say more than my words ever will..

Lost
by Ryan Woods

I began to disappear
long before I became lost...
Piece, by precious piece,
I vanished...
As you counted the days
And I counted the cost,
and waited for the fog to lift

Life is a gift
that we should savour...
Though its flavour
may not always be to our taste
Because, sometimes
in our haste, we forget to season it
With love
and with laughter

And all the while,
the hereafter
promises redemption
for our failures,
which haunt us like ghosts

Most of all,
I miss my innocence;
and my carefree ways,
before my days
became smothered
by anxiety

And though piety,
was never my strong point,
if I could anoint myself
with Holy water
to draw out these demons,
I surely would

They say that,
good things come to he who waits,
So, I wait...

But, salvation is not forthcoming...
Numbing my ills
with booze and pills
is only a temporary solution
It is absolution,
that I seek...

Blessed are the meek,
for they shall inherit the earth…

My self-worth,
has dropped below zero...
And whilst I was never the hero,
that you wanted
At times,
I was the monster
that you needed

In that role,
at least,
I succeeded

The memories
which I once followed like breadcrumbs
to help me find my way home,
now lay scattered
to the four winds
and I am consigned to oblivion

Each day I walk a tightrope,
that spans a cavernous maw
which waits for me to lose
my grip
on reality

and slip,
evermore
into the abyss

And as I fall,
I close my eyes;
thinking that somehow
that will keep out the darkness
But, how can I hope to keep out,
that which has already found a home
inside of me…

Fifty Shades of Mediocrity
by Ryan Woods

Drowning, alone
In my moments of mediocrity
There is no life preserver,
to save me from sinking
into the dark depths of despair

Depression has made its lair
deep inside of me,
where it festers, like cancer

I wait,
for my prayers to be answered
But it seems
that I have been forsaken

Taken,
for granted;
I have recanted all that I once held dear…

And now, my fear of the unknown
has sown
seeds of self-doubt in my mind,
which have taken root,
and are flourishing
in the fertile soil of my inadequacy

My failure
in the roles that I have chosen
has frozen me to the core…
Evermore,
making me feel like a shell
of my former self

I am only half the man
that I used to be
And only a tenth of the man

that I wish I was
Because, each day
I slip further into the quagmire
that drags me under

This is no Wonderland…
It is a place of broken promises
and shattered dreams
A place where my screams
fall on deaf ears
And my fears
rise, like mountains in my path

And in the aftermath
I sit and count the ways
in which I have failed…

Derailed, and devalued
My life has lost its meaning
And whilst I tried my best
to colour it in all the hues of the rainbow
I only succeed in painting it
in fifty shades of mediocrity.

Next stop…Nowhere!
by Ryan Woods

I awaken
to the sounds of birds chirping…
How dare they be so cheerful?
Their carefree chorus seems like mockery

Fearful
of what lies ahead,
I rise
even though I despise
every minute that I spend awake
and every breath that I take
only fuels the nightmare
that I have awoken unto

My dreams,
long shattered
like windows in an abandoned building
My memories,
ghosts from happier times,
haunt me, still…
gloating at the wretchedness
of my existence

Persistence,
seems futile
So, I while away the hours
in a haze…

Dazed and confused,
I feel like yesterday's news
A tabloid sob story
of wasted opportunities
and bad choices

I wish that I could put to bed
the voices in my head

because they are an infection
But like my reflection,
I cannot escape them

So, I simply continue
to put one foot
in front of the other
even though I know
that my next stop
is nowhere…

After the Rain
by Sahana Mukherjee

A web of cobs carries
the ashes of my cigarettes.
I think of you mostly through
a blue screen translucent as
a frosted window glass, but you
are in water, and me, I'll
never come close to such wealth.

Sending my Father Home
by Sahana Mukherjee

The moon wanes on your shoulder
as you walk with your scythe.
Homebound, barely. You must
bury the night. A herd of sheep
once knew you. You carried
your home on their backs.

Now, time slips from the creases
of your fist. You stroll about and
around. You let your father kiss

Fire thrice, and cry and cry
over spilt milk.

Dream Stealer
by Sarah Battison

It is only when light fades and the shadows appear from the impending darkness that I surface,
The heaviness of the night crushes the dreams of civilians and I am the curse that steals your souls.

I am devoid of feeling, missing my humanity and incapable of knowing love,
When the blackness settles I emerge from the shadows.

I am the nastiest nightmare,
I am your lonely, deepest despair.

I will encompass every worry, every tear,
You are mine.

The darkness feeds me,
Your dreams entice me,
I am the dream stealer,
I will turn your nightmares into reality.

I am the embodiment of bleak, unforgiving, un-healing depressions

I come out of the darkness,
Tip-toeing and residing in the darkest, deepest depths of your soul.

Jagged Blankets of Depression
by Sarah Battison

A jagged blanket of depression, its fabric wrapped in stinging nettles.
Everything's okay as long as I don't offer any resistance, but if I do, there's hell to pay.
Each movement and the stinging nettles slide across my scarred and sunken skin.
Each movement is painful, a poor attempt at fighting the depressive wave of blanketed bleakness, but sometimes it devours me.

My depression is a stone, thrown at the bottom of a dark ocean. It's stuck there with no escape.

My depression is a lonely cloud that wonders desperately through the darkness of the night, searching for the things it is yet to find.

It is a ball, a ball of unachieved aspirations and of delusional dreams.

I am broken.
As broken as the glass from a shattered vase that bounces across an empty room.
As broken as the wounds that you have left etched into my very soul.

I am lonely.
My depression tells me I want to be alone in a dark room with nobody else there but my heart tells me I AM LONELY.

I am but a combination of the words etched into my skin from everyone else,
I am but a combination of all the broken promises and whispered lies of love.

I am nothing but a combination of the empty dreams and aspirations that have been left in the waiting room in the back of my mind.

My anxiety tells every night to crawl into the pit of death that swallows me whole,
that digs its sharp talons into my body and wraps me in its arms of loneliness.

Each morning I struggle against the grasp of depression and fight my way out of bed.

My depression is a bottle. With the cap screwed tightly shut. Each shake of my inner thoughts and the fizz begins to rise.
The pressure gets harder. But there is no escape as the bottle top of my mouth is screwed so tightly shut that nothing can escape.

My depression is a battle.
It is a tennis match between the two voices that appear in my head.
It is a snooker game of balls that roll around with different numbers, each one representing the thoughts that slide around my brain.
It is a bus full of people taking the long ride out of town, talking at the same time, chatting at the same time, crying at the same time.

It is a football field with no footballers.

My mind is a waiting room full of patients yet to be seen.
It's full of diseases that have been contaminated by the spread of evil,
of hate,
of destruction.

My Brain is a battlefield.
Full of war wounds and scars, new wars beginning every.. single... day.
Of all the wishes and whispers of yesterday's desires.

Its nerves shattered with shell shock from the bullet like words that left your mouth.

Your mouth was the weapon of my mass destruction.
An atomic bomb of emotional abuse of making more than one excuse, of doing unimaginable things to my heart.

My smile is held together with puppet strings.
Depression is the puppeteer.
It decides when I smile, when I laugh, when I cry.
It decides when I can no longer speak - muffled voices bounce across the inside of my lips.

My anxiety tells me that every single person in this room is quietly judging the lumps and bumps of my body.
My anxiety tells me to forewarn my friend - "film me, but try not to make me look fat".
My anxiety tells me to take a picture at 20 different angles.
My anxiety tells me that each person I meet will judge my skin.
My anxiety tells me that eating in front of people is a big mistake because my anxiety tells me that they will be thinking she doesn't need to eat ... she's fat enough.

But you know what?
You know how I shut that monotonous voice of anxiety up?
By comfort eating.
By devouring chocolate like my life depends on it.
That small bit of dopamine makes my adrenaline soar, makes my mood lift and makes me smile.

For about 20 seconds anyway.

And then.
Like clockwork.
My snake like inner subconscious recoils within itself, my voice - like a tiny whisper amongst a sea of sadness, she says "you've done it again Sarah. Now look how fat you'll get "
My anxiety tells me everything.

My anxiety is the judgemental shadow that follows me around, she clings to my every single move, my every thought.
She is everywhere.

My heart was like a mirror.
It was beaten with a hammer, each time smashed to pieces. Each time I fixed the mirror within me.
Each time it was fixed in vain. Each time the reflection is distorted.
Next time the hammer was bigger, this time the pieces were smaller, still I super glued the glass of my heart together again. Reflections even more distorted, again - fixed in vain.

My poor, battered, broken heart.

I am overcome with sadness, but my depression tells me that my heart is empty,
that my emotions are dark and bleak and that the only emotion I am allowed is fear.

Fear of continual survival.
The fear of expectation.
The fear of being honest,
The fear of repetition.

But yet, my depression does NOT allow me time to breathe or time to think about my own rhetorical questions.

It has become nothing but an impossible essay question, an unimaginable task of searching for answers and being left with no words to find...
Just nothing.

I am but the combination of all this anxiety.
I wear it like a scarf every single day.
It restricts my breathing when the scarf of anxiety pulls itself too tightly around my neck, it keeps my body warm with its constant niggling, even though inside my body is freezing cold.
Like ice.

I am the victim of bullying,
I am the victim of rape,
I am the victim of drug abuse - both as a user and an observer.
I am a victim of Domestic Abuse.
I am a victim.

I am a combination of my experiences.

I am a combination.
I am strange, I am broken, and I am not someone who everyone can love.
But look within me and you'll see that my broken, tainted soul is beautiful.

My anxiety tells me you'll laugh at that.
My anxiety tells me that I shouldn't be standing up here right now.

But for the first time in a long time - I'm doing the exact opposite of what my anxiety tells me.

People often ask, Are you okay? I say yeah, I'm fine. I'm okay...

IM NOT FINE AND IM NOT OKAY.

My brain is a constant battle every, single, day.
Don't believe a single word that I will often say because my depression, my anxiety, that's what makes me this way.

I'm standing in a busy town centre.
I'm screaming at the top of my lungs and not one person reacts,
then I realise that my lips are sealed shut,
the screams muffled,
no noise,
just imperfect silence.

No one can hear me, because I cannot find the words to tell you.

Are you okay Sarah? NO!

My depression is the tepid water that surrounds me.
It gives you the promise of warmth but only when you submerge yourself fully under, do you realise how cold it is.

The water laps at my body reminding me of every scar of every open wound.
The water devours me , and it's my anxiety that tells me ,
it tells me - shouts at me - it says -
"STOP TRYING TO STAY AFLOAT. STOP KEEPING YOUR HEAD ABOVE THE WATER. LET GO"

The promise of my children's future is the only thing that keeps my head afloat.
It is the only thing that keeps my body above the water.
It is the only thing that reminds me to be strong,
the only thing that tells me to carry on.

If I didn't have this amazing love in my body, in my bones for my children...
I'd let the water pull me in.

I'd let the water pull me down.

I would let it take me to the darkest deepest depths and I would let it devour me.

And.

I would drown.

I'd drown.

F you anxiety. I did it anyway.

Destruction
by Sarah Battison

Hope is destroyed
And my life burnt
As my soul relishes in the flames of your darkest mistakes.

The wisps of smoke cloud my judgement,
I find myself thinking about you.

You are just one in this world.
One person who singlehandedly nearly took down a whole family.
I'd even wrote suicide notes to my 9-year-old daughter.

You were somehow able to strip my body of a choice,
You somehow contaminated my thoughts with your voice,
You were able to control my actions, my desires,
And in all of that, your wishes you conspired.

A bleak, black darkness had settled, clouds formed over my head,
And I sat there every day telling you how I wanted to be dead,
How I couldn't live anymore with the constricting pain,
How if you left I'd find it hard to love again.

Your hands around my throat,
Strong and constricting,
Merciless and restricting.

The darkness has lifted, the light finally appears,
I'm just glad it only took me months - and not years.
Any longer with the weight of your contributed pain,

And I would probably never have opened my eyes again.

Dirty Thoughts
by Sarah Dale

Dirty thoughts are worse
than graffiti in the underpass
stinking of piss, vomit, cigarettes.

You need more than a bucket and a mop.
A dammed river would be useful,
perhaps a lake of fire,
a suicide bomber,
an earthquake –
something serious and terminal.

Once the brain is gone
and the bone smashed to ash
still the writing to get rid of,
and the books.

**Twisting and Breaking
by Sarah Dale**

If you had ever listened
you would have heard the sound
when my heart broke.
It was a quiet noise
that made no practical difference.

So, I twisted you
round my finger
till you broke.
Now I'll plant you
and water you
and when you start to shoot
again, with fresh green leaves
I'll twist you
round my little finger
till you break.

I've watched and waited,
so, I heard the sound
when your heart broke.
It was a quiet noise
that made no practical difference.

The Ice Cave
by Shaun Gurmin

Rigid and cold,
I sat in the ice cave,
surrounded by crystals:
how easily I could see through them,
their emptiness,
merely reflecting what they were not.

I searched, longing for warmth,
longing for substance.
In a crevice, I found something,
radiant, a burning piece of amber.
It wasn't transparent like the others.
It was rich with colour, rich with power.
I sat there and gazed, at its beauty,
its inner universe of galaxies,
of yellows and oranges, bursting within.

Something started to appear.
Slowly, I could see.
There I was: happy, bright, glowing, warm.
Enchanted, I wondered if this was my reflection.
But with time, the fiery gem darkened,
and became as cold and blank as the other stones.
Desperately, I ran from rock to rock, cavern to cavern,
in search of myself.

I knew I was different from those crystal caskets.
I knew I had substance. I saw it: I saw the light inside.
Wanting to see it again, I ventured into forbidden land,
beyond the mouth of the ice cave.

Outside, the bright skies scorched me.
Gradually, I felt myself tiring, until I could no longer walk.
I glanced down and noticed droplets,
melting and merging, on the ground before me.
I looked into the pool.

Sparkling, glowing, refracting colours, I saw myself.
I was beautiful: yellows, blues, greens, and reds.

Weakening, I dropped towards my reflection,
tears fleeing my seared surface.
Disturbing the charm, agitating the clarity,
The final drop rippled the water.
Then, I saw that the beauty and colours,
were just phantom refractions,
from a melting crystal mirror.

Black Tears
by Shaun Gurmin

As I struggle along this path,
sharp thorns tear through my flesh,
insects sting, and serpents bite.

I become hungry and weak, famished.
I eat the first thing I see; a blue apple,
and quickly spit out a mouthful of worms and maggots.

A toxin burns like a fire beneath my skin,
sindering the nerves, removing my ability to touch and feel.
Flowing through the veins, a black toxic poison,
invading and destroying everything from the inside out:
stealing me, involuntary shocks,
breathing rapidly, heart beating faster,
sweating, delirious.

I drag myself along the trail,
rocks piercing into my wounds,
insects breeding their spawn,
and laying their eggs in the gashes of my flesh.
I persist, no sense of direction,
just fulfilling my body´s final function.

As I roll over and start convulsing,
a branch hangs overhead - with two apples,
one blue and one green.
I fight to overcome my body´s desire,
to wither and rot into the earth beneath me.
I watch as my bloodied, bruised and infected arm,
rises up and away from me.
Shaking, retreating but then returning,
it continues to the green apple.
I watch as my hand grasps on to the apple,
expecting to be able to feel its delicate skin,
its blemishes, imperfections,
as well as its texture and ripeness,
but nothing.

I remain in silence,

watching my hand numbly hold a green apple,
and listening to my flesh being devoured,
screaming to be ripped away from my bones,
welcoming a less painful death,
of passing through the intestines of the forest scavengers,
rather than persist with the fire of the venom,
invading my body,
penetrating every living cell.

I bring the apple down closer,
and smell its sweet aroma,
exciting a part of my brain still wishing to live.
One bite, but I taste nothing,
like chewing crunchy foam.
I swallow in haste,
bits of unchewed apple pass through
my dehydrated and corroded throat,
like shards of glass.

Shortly after, I start to feel warm inside,
maybe due to nerves firing,
causing a sensation of heat;
something good flows through my veins.

My heart stops.
And for an eternity,
I lie there,
suspended in time.

With a shock through my body,
my heart restarts,
purging out the damage and pain,
and breathing in clean air;
crying venom,
black tears race away from my eyes.

I look up,
noticing all the green apples.

Delhi 2004
by Sravani Singampalli

I still remember those days
When I used to chase butterflies
While my mother used to
Boil my favourite sweet potatoes
Those days when
We used to enjoy selling
Piles of old newspapers
And all the empty wine bottles
To the scrap dealer
Whom we used to call a 'kabadiwala'
For money and sometimes for
Masala papads and potato chips.
I miss the days
When we used to
Secretly enter Uncle Paul's garden
Start plucking flowers and
Those sour tangerines.
Sometimes I really feel awkward
When I remember how I used to
Steal pencils and sharpeners.
I miss so many things
Those chilly winter mornings
The chirping of petite tree sparrows
The smell of happy childhood
The air of freedom.

Life is a Glass of Coke
by Sravani Singampalli

I sit with a glass of coke
I take small sips
And enjoy it's refreshing taste.
Conversations with my friends press on
And after sometime
When I start taking another sip
It no longer tastes refreshing
No longer like coke
But like a tea decoction.
The coke lost its effervescence
Just like our extended conversations
Just like our cheeks and skin
Just like our behaviour.
The conversations become meaningless
Skin loses its elasticity
And we become forlorn citizens.

Front Page of the Express and Star
by Stevie Quick

Standing by the tram tracks
Not looking back; waiting for the tram car
Going to make the front page of the Express and Star.
And all the ones who hate me
Will all line up to praise me
And I'll go from being a problem
To being a beautiful talented student
With loads of potential and a good prospect
you'll show me respect, you'll put flowers
where I was, you'll stop calling me names no it won't be
the same you'll just find some other kid to shame you
will you bastards you know you will.
I wonder which picture my mum will choose for the
papers and midlands today to use, the one where I was seven and full
of hope and smiles or the last one when
all the miles I travelled show up on my face,
I'm twelve I'm staring at the camera like a zombie 'cause on the
other side they're all laughing at me:
Laughing at me and the teachers wouldn't see and you
couldn't see and I was screaming for me and nobody
heard I felt like a bird standing in the road as car races
towards it.
Trams leave this stop every 10 minutes. on the hour,
then ten past, twenty past half past, twenty to and ten
to..
I'm ten minutes down the line.
Start counting
Ten; stay alive, what then?
Nine; pretend it's still fine?
Eight: don't wait up Mum, gonna be late.
Seven; do I go to heaven?
Six; pick up sticks don't know why its what my nan says
Five; still alive.
Four; or..?
Three; Still think you can save me?
Two; Know what to do?
One; I'm gone.

That my Name
by Stevie Quick

That my name.
It belong me.
I did not give it to you
To put on your tongue;
To shout out loud;
I did not give it to you
To call me out
To use it wrong.

This my name
It belong me;
It is who I am
It is me;
I can use it
I can shout out loud
I have it on my tongue
I can use it wrong

This my name
Do not presume to use it:
It is not for your tongue.
It is not made for your mouth;
Shut your lips.
Still your tongue.
Do not even whisper it.

If, if, I ever give it you,
You may say thank you.

What Does it Mean to be a Human?
by Sunayna Pal

What does it mean to be a human?

Organs hands and legs?
A dead body has it too.
A soul and mind?
Plants have it too.

A live body with soul?
Animals have it too.

What does it really mean to be a human?
Isn't it the ability to forgive
to help
to cooperate
to laugh
to cry

and most important of all
To love.

The Flood
by Taylor Bain

Thunderheads boil over my mind's desert,
Pouring raw emotion
Into the dry cracks of its parched earth.

I stagger to my ark,
Built to house my rationality.
I will be safe here,
Tending to my hollow memories.

Flame
by Taylor Bain

His anger burns me.
My brain blisters in the heat.
I taste love's ashes.

Social Anxiety
by Taylor Bain

Strangers are painful,
They tear into my psyche,
Oblivious thorns.

Eclipsed
by Tina Cole

I've been thinking of the things you said
the day we watched the eclipse,
about that house where pollarded trees
clubbed out the sun
& so many sharp things under foot
with only an old Hoover
coughing its own death rattle to protect you.

The long shadows cast
by that lumpy woman
who made you call her mother,
treadling through shallow pocketed days
with a lolling tongue of tape measure
at her neck & needles at her breast.

The mockery
of those Instamatic smiles;
you dandified in her latest creations,
spontaneity zipped by everyday
snappy rejoinders,
it was no wonder you began to fray.

I see now
she made you orbit her sun
in a world where the moon
would always look harried
long before the darkness set in.

Yesterday when I knocked,
her wobbling silhouette filled the frame;
still spitting out insults,
she laughed when I spoke of you
and as the door slammed
a thin wedge of light glowed red.

Shell
by Tina Cole

I cupped you to my ear
waiting for a voice
but only heard whispers
in lap, slap, splattering tones.

I wanted the breathless
suck and roar
but there was only emptiness
& the crosshatched bar codes,

of a reddening tide..

Infamy
by Tina Manthorpe

There must have been a time,
a time before these names of people,
places, were of universal significance,
bywords for evil and destruction.

A time of innocent infancy
for young Adolf
and golden-haired Myra,
son and daughter of ordinary parents,
no doubt.

At one time, Edge Hill and Spion Kop
were simply landmarks,
geographical features
unconnected with battle and death;
Dachau and Auschwitz towns, villages,
innocuous before their ignominy.

Once, you could have walked
on Saddleworth Moor
without shuddering, enjoying
the simple pleasures of clean air,
and rain-washed skies.

How many years must elapse
before the untimely dead are forgotten,
as the drifts of bodies around Maiden Castle,
and the severed heads adorning
the earthen ramparts on beautiful Bredon
have vanished from our collective memories?

Lindow Man
by Tina Manthorpe

Submissively
he stood, naked, before them,
well-built, well-breakfasted.
He bowed his head,
in consent

and they hit him once,
felling him to the ground.
They hit him twice,
fracturing his skull,
perhaps killing him.

They lifted his limp body,
his perfect body,
clad with a single adornment,
his fox-fur emblem
around his arm, they lifted him
and throttled him

pulling tight the thug's garrotte
around his neck, suffocating,
if he had in fact any breath left.
They slashed his throat,
spurting carotid's blood
a scarlet fountain
in the moorland air.
He fell, lifeless, naked,
they dragged him to the water,
placed him face downwards,
left him to rot.

Was he a priest, a victim?
A sacrifice?
Was this retribution,
punishment
for unimaginable crimes? Was he willing,

proud to be chosen?
Was he guaranteed a better life?
Will we ever know?

Will he ever be nameless,
known simply as Lindow man?

**Le Pays Noir
by William A Douglas Davies**

J M W Turner saw this.
Their Apocalypse, then; c.1832.
Black, red, black, red...
black by day, red by night.
Except...
No ecstasy, save exploitation.
No passion, only pain.
Twisted Chelsea masters' poverty porn;
Vile, filthy City gambling-whores.

Hard men; crooked, broken
on the wheels of industry.
What's the price of progress?
My grandfather's words of ignorance and disease echo in my
head.

Just Before
by William A Douglas Davies

What was it like before impact?
Was it gruesome, horrifying and loud?
Did the sea part with huge rents?
Were the skies filled with terrible clouds?
Did fire spew from the ground like Armageddon?
Or was it quiet? Deathly, like a black bottomless pit?
Airless and choking?
Or was it serene?
I know...

L'Addition
by William A Douglas Davies

I thought that once
I had touched the face of God,
but fooled by a colourless rainbow
I had danced with the devil.
This sick joke spiralled into damned attrition.
Unaware of any bargain
until Hell's bailiff called;
the price I was told was my soul.
Desperately I gazed from this macabre fix.
Crossing The Styx I spat Charon's coin out
Terrified; so late I swam towards the light.
A sudden moment of change
brought violent paroxysms.
Tectonic plates slipped abruptly;
awesome waves crashed, the Earth shook.
Echoes of my unpaid debt reverberated.

Paranoid
by Xtina Marie

I hear the whispers
see the shadows lurk
tell myself
this sanity's work

What is real?
What is truth?
I need some help
my soul to soothe

The veil is thin
dreams aren't lucid
rotting flesh
the smell is putrid

I hear the screams
inside my mind
focus on words
that used to rhyme

I see the eyes
follow room to room
they envelope me
as mother's womb

I tear at my face
rip out hair
know in my heart
the monsters aren't there

But they stare at me
with their soulless eyes
and reach out
as if I'm the prize

They won't leave me be
I huddle in the corner
at my sanity's funeral
I'm the lone mourner

I follow to the gravesite
give death a little flirt
pick up the shovel
my hands caked with dirt

I climb into the hole
sanity destroyed
forgetting for a moment
I'm just paranoid

We'll Rendezvous
by Xtina Marie

Lulled to sleep
by the sound of your breathing
my subconscious knows
you're the dream that I'm dreaming

Surrounded by you
you cloud all my days
I walk around serene
in a love induced haze

I close my eyes and I'm there
we're the only ones in this land
we walk side-by-side
through a field, hand-in-hand

I stop to pull you close
and plant a kiss on your lips
we need no special glasses
to see the magic in this eclipse

With your hand in my hair
you start to work your charms
but don't you know, darling?
everything I'll ever want is in your arms

We make love by the water
listening to the still of a pond
the beauty is all around us
as if waved by a fairy's wand

After- we lay there
our breathing labored and spent
I nibble lazily at your shoulder
thoroughly content

You tell me you love me
and I smile at the words
the most beautiful sound there is
rivaling the songs of the birds

Day turns to night
turns back to day
and I know the thing I dread the most
I'm about to hear you say

You bid me farewell
I'm your favorite dream girl
and you promise we'll rendezvous
again tonight in our dream world

His Muse
by Xtina Marie

He calls me his muse
but I'm more like his albatross
I suppose in life
we all bear our cross

I want to be his light
shining through the dark
instead I'm the stray cat
he befriended in the park

I want to be the joy
when the all the world is bleak
but I'm the black coffee
when what he wanted was weak

I want to be the sparkle
in his warm brown eyes
instead I'm the thunder
and the darkening skies

I want to be the song
that he sings in the shower
but I'm more like the weeds
in a garden that never flowers

I want to be his comfort
when it's cold and it rains
but instead I'm his annoyance
like an achy joint that only pains

I want to be his laughter
when he gets too serious
but I'm the horror book
creepy and mysterious

I want to be his heaven
but I fear I'm his hell
I'll lead him to the darkness
where we'll be locked in my cell

I want to be his passion
that's never satisfied
but I'm more like his poison
and the sweet taste of cyanide

I want to be his forever
sealed with a kiss
instead I'm his prison
guarded by the serpent's hiss.

The Parcel
by Yolanda Barton

The morning after
it's cast upon the table,
the parcel, crisp and crackling
carelessly angled
plainly swathed
and unmarked.

The words within
ripped from his throat
like tape off paper, a delivery
over which she has no rights
statutory or otherwise
and cannot return.

Before she could protest
that the address was wrong,
that the contents were not
what she had asked for,
the door had slammed
and she heard the final growl of his van.

The clock crawls forward.
She makes black coffee,
cups her face in hands.
The parcel sits unopened,
unlooked-at,
obtrusive, squat.

Dragging it to the shops,
red-eyed, so easy to leave it
inside, by the stammering till clerk,
who takes it on break,
fails to call out the bomb squad
and hides it away

until later, outside the bar
where the girls squall
at the folded-armed security guard
as somehow it spills
outward to the floor
splattered like spit on the pavement.

Apocalypse, Possibly
by Yolanda Barton

At some time, after finding the milk
like the Titanic's iceberg in the freezer,
Or one whole week of lentil soup
brewed like potion with cut-price sausages,
Or me collapsed on the floor, my blood's iron rusted away,
My lovers have been reminded
suffering's scar never leaves.
But *in A World*
Where One Man is defined by pain,
The challenge of my survival must be met with contempt.
Then the men who've shared my bed will scry the future,
And reply with their fantasy apocalypse.

The cause is always different.
Perhaps it is the fall of the European Union,
Or an older Union, our country,
Or the sickened earth will repel us, unleashing a swarm of plagues,
Or China will attack.
The seas are poisoned, or else
Nuclear waste leaks onto the good soil.
Mass extinction skips hand in hand
With North Korea unleashing VX
And Germans punishing us for Brexit.
God announces his existence as solely God of wrath
In petulant defiance of Scripture.
The Islamists, against all logic, might take control
(Bad news for a conservative,
Who would take up arms in his soft, unworked fingers;
Good news for the modern leftist,
Who dons a fashionable checked scarf,
Smokes shisha with his new friends,
And goes out to tend his allotment.)

This is definitely coming, they say.
Therefore, there is no point in going out today,
But it is philosophically right to sit on the sofa
And await the end, playing their console.
They are waiting for the start of a Hans Zimmer soundtrack
And to be the apocalyptic hero.
And as for my dreams of writing books
And next year when I'll see how tall my Taiwanese godson's grown?

Forget it. Nobody will want to read
Or love foreigners in the abyss when the world has ended.
Ambition is trivial, I'm told;
But anyway, *what do I think?*

There is no response.
It's the death of conversation,
The ultimate negation
Of hope, their words hanging
In silence like lines of the lynched.

And where am I,
Where do I fit in this image?
Prone.
Uncomplicated now, lying listless
On a slab, or in a ditch,
With silenced questions in my blank eyes.
Or cloaked beneath a veil of cloth,
A veil of dirt, or poverty, or malnutrition
That at long last
Has drained the impudent blood from my cheeks.

The coffin in their vision
Is that of catalyst.
Don't I know someone has to spark
Our hero's righteous rage?
Don't I know that in the wasteland,
There must be someone to avenge?

So, it would be with me. And with this new status
Dreams, goals, desires I had,
Arguments over career, destiny, taste,
All are gone. There is no negotiation with a dead girl.
The Last Man stands alone on a howling crag,
His face brooding beneath slick hair
And stubble growing just so for his unknown audience.
Derbyshire rock beneath him
Reaches for the poison rain.
The credits, at long last, roll in,
A portentous swell of thunder's cannon fire.

Disco Tent
by Z D Dicks

Now is the winter of our disco tent
Our smoking havens
To escape late rent
To laugh and bray
To come what may
Stay up late and make a world pay

Now is our winter of our disco tent
Our rent is due
Our wages spent
So, we will stand in the cold
Smoking cheap fags
Ignoring our pain
Our waterproof boots deflecting the rain

Now is the winter of our disco tent
Where we will cry in the dark
At our hopes
And our wages
Poorly spent

Unseen Entity
by Z D Dicks

I am the monster that is harboured in your head
Not under stairs
Or in your bed
You feed me daily with each negative thought
Make me stronger and enriched when you are most distraught
I have no pity
Or any shame
I laugh because you take the blame
I am a little voice not a separate voice
The narrative of every choice
I have your conscience silenced and bound
At three o' clock I like to surface
Remind you of what is lost and never found
Again
I am the monster harboured in your head
I will live here always until you are dead.

Portrait
by Z D Dicks

The Queen's face,
is no longer gluten free,
plastic like a supermodel,
and smaller in stature.
It's harder for her to crease up,
but when she does,
she stays folded,
and bent.

London is now transparent,
and only bright reflections,
stand out.
Nobody is interested in the other side,
the flip-side.
The keen eyed watch,
for the forgery,
where London used to be,
as it has no value.
A cheap knock-off,
that pretends to represent something.

Bouteille
by Zoe Alford

I was the water
that clung to your neck and sides
moulded myself to your shape.
She was the heavy sand
who, unnoticed,
slipped into your hidden spaces
and sucked the life from me.
All the while
you held us both
within the glass walls of your heart.

Gregor
by Zoe Alford

In the end
you survive the heartache
as a hardened roach
only survivor
of a torched world
burnt anew.

You may wince at the sight of yourself
as others do
perennially squashed
in warm stale ridges
of duvet
drenched in tears
and sweat
as ashes slide from your back
the dying embers of a dream.

Now the trial is over
you slick back your black shell
emerging triumphant
from wreckage of another man's home
in your true and final form.

Introducing the cover artist….

David Nicholls is an artist, poet and aspiring writer. His home is currently the tranquil Isle of Portland in Dorset. It is here he set up his business, White Stones Art Café, which is now well established and is popular with locals and visitors alike. Anyone taking time to visit this unique space will find David's art studio located in the peaceful café gardens. It is from here he creates the unique mosaic artwork, illustrated on the cover of this book. Alongside his art studio are three Eco friendly holiday studios, where visitors can come to stay and take part in one of his mosaic workshops if they wish.

David's original artistic direction was that of sculpture but a trip to Barcelona and time spent living in Southern Spain has seen his work take a whole new direction. He has work in private and public collections and often works to commission.

In between all this David tries to put pen to paper as often as possible and is currently working on a fantasy fiction novel. He has only more recently turned his hand to poetry and in a brief time has proudly become a published poet. This new venture into poetry has seen him explore many different topics, some very personal, some dark and some much lighter hearted and humorous. There is usually an underlying message or point to his work, even if it is not immediately apparent.

David is a member of a local writing group called Portland Pens and various online poetry groups such as nOthing BOOKS – Poetry Collective of the Diverse, Gloucester Poetry Society, Rusty Goats Poetry Corner and it here he posts his work regularly.

Facebook & Instagram: davidnichollsart
www.whitestonesstudios.com
Facebook & Instagram: whitestonesstudios
www.whitestonescafe.com
Facebook: WhiteStones Easton
Instagram: whitestonesartcafe
Facebook: Portland Pens

within darkness & light
a collection of poetry

compiled by
paul b morris

Available to buy on Amazon.co.uk & Amazon.com

Made in the USA
Columbia, SC
31 October 2018